Professional English in Use

Law

Gillian D. Brown
Sally Rice

Thanks and acknowledgments

Thanks to our families, friends and colleagues for their understanding, interest and assistance. Thanks are due to Nicholas Robinson and Antoinette Meehan for their dedicated editorial work and to the production team at Cambridge University Press. Thanks in particular go to the Institute for Applied Language Studies (University of Edinburgh) and Michelmores Solicitors for their support.

The publisher would like to thank Dorthe Engelhardt, Ian Chisholm and Monica Hoogstad for reviewing the material prior to publication. Thanks also to John Dovey from The Takeover Panel.

The authors and publishers are grateful to the following for permission to reproduce copyright material. While every effort has been made, it has not always been possible to identify the sources of all the material used, or to contact the copyright holders. If any omissions are brought to our notice, we will be happy to include the appropriate acknowledgements on reprinting.

The Council of Tribunals for the Report of Council on Tribunals on p. 20; The Office of Public Sector Information for the adapted text on p. 36 from 'The Money Laundering Regulations 2003'; Plain English Campaign for the adapted text on p. 43; The Office of Government Commerce (OGC) for the adapted text on p. 57, Annex B: Extract from the OGC Model Agreements, © Crown Copyright; The Takeover Panel for the text on p. 61 adapted from 'Summary of the Provisions of Rule 8'; The Times for the text on p. 61, ' Linde offers £138m to ease delay in BOC bid' by Peter Klinger, 7 March 2006, © N I Syndication; The Guardian for the adapted material on p. 63, 'Supermarket competition inquiry may break stranglehold of big four', by Julia Finch and Felicity Lawrence, 10 March 2006, © Guardian Newspapers Limited; Oxford University Press for the adapted letter on p. 65 from The Oxford Handbook of Legal Correspondence, ed, Rupert Haigh, © Oxford University Press, 2006; Blackstone Press for the material on p. 69 from Blackstone's LLB learning texts: law of contract © Oxford University Press, 1996; Practical Law Company for extract on p. 85, 'Break clauses for leases' from www.practicallaw.com; Tim Buckingham for the adapted text on p. 95, 'Pharming is taking over from phishing' by Tim Buckingham, 16 August 2005; Cambridge University Press for the promotional material on Principles of International Environmental Law by Philippe Sands on p. 97.

The publishers are grateful to the following for permission to reproduce copyright photographs and material:

Key: l = left, c = centre, r = right, t = top, b = bottom

Alamy Images / ©Alex Segre for p. 14, ©David Hoffman Photo Library for p. 16, ©Mike Abrahams for p. 26, ©Glow Images for p. 27, ©Eyebyte for p. 58, ©Justin Kase for p. 60(t), ©Alex Beaton for p. 60(b), ©Photofusion Picture Library for p. 87, ©Michael Booth for p. 84; Corbis / ©Tom Grill for p. 19, ©Blend Images for p. 24(b), ©Zefa/Pinto for p. 29, ©Zefa/Alan Schein for p. 49(r), ©Pixland for p. 62, ©Zefa/Roy McMahon for p. 80, ©Colorblind for p. 82, ©John Noble for p. 97; Getty Images / ©Riser for p. 12(t), ©Taxi for p. 24(t), ©Stone for p. 34, ©Image Bank for p. 45(l), ©Stone for p. 49(l); LexisNexis Butterworths for p. 12(b); Punchstock / ©Digital Vision for p. 18, ©PhotoDisc for p. 25, ©Brand X for p. 28, ©Digital Vision for p. 45(r), ©Brand X for p. 56, ©Tetra Images for p. 66, ©Stockbyte for p. 71, ©Blend Images for p. 74, ©Blend Images for p. 86, ©PhotoDisc for p. 94; Rex for pp. 17, 31; The Stationery Office Ltd for p. 11; www.eoc.org.uk and www.paulineneild.co.uk for p. 20.

Picture research by Hilary Luckcock.

Disclaimer

This publication is intended for the sole and exclusive purpose of providing legal English instruction and is sold with the understanding that the publishers and authors are not engaged in providing legal advice. None of the information in this publication is intended to constitute, nor does it constitute, legal advice. Consequently, the contents of this publication should not be regarded as constituting legal advice or guidance, should not be relied upon for providing legal advice, guidance or recommendations to any third party, and should not under any circumstances be used in lieu of the advice of a qualified lawyer.

Contents

Introduction

Who is this book for?

Professional English in Use Law is for a wide range of people who need to use legal English vocabulary in their work, for example as lawyers or litigators, paralegals or legal researchers, legal secretaries or trainee lawyers. English language learners may need to use legal English to work with foreign colleagues or clients; to describe or explain aspects of their own legal system; to find out about other systems. The book is also for students of law who wish to develop their knowledge of legal English vocabulary to assist their legal studies. It will also help extend the vocabulary of business professionals who need some knowledge of legal English vocabulary for commercial agreements and transactions. The book is suitable for learners who have reached an upper-intermediate or advanced level of English. The book can be used effectively for individual study or by a teacher in class, one to one or in groups. If you are preparing for the ILEC exam (*International Legal English Certificate*), this book will help you to develop your vocabulary.

Language and law

The book aims to help learners develop their legal English vocabulary. It is not intended to be an introduction to law in English speaking countries nor to be relied upon for information or advice about law or the practice of law. It presents vocabulary in the context of the legal systems in the UK because the meaning of any legal terms and the conceptual relationship between terms is located within a specific legal system. The authors assume that you will need to talk and write about your own legal system. Consequently, some tasks encourage you to think about how far your own system shares the same legal concepts or procedures, and to decide whether to use a legal term in English as an equivalent to a concept in your own system or to employ an approximation in discussion or writing (see Unit 17).

What kind of legal English is in this book?

This book concentrates on the vocabulary arising from the practice of commercial law (including company law, contract formation, employment law, sale of goods, real property, and intellectual property) but also presents more general legal English vocabulary. The legal topics covered are common to many legal systems and in that context the book has an international dimension. There are references in most units of the book to English language websites to help you to extend your language practice and to assist your understanding of legal concepts in English in authentic contexts.

How is the book organised?

The book consists of 45 two-page units organised into four thematic sections: **The legal system, Legal professionals, Legal professionals in practice,** and **Law in practice** (including **Liability, Contract, Intellectual property, Information technology law,** and **Environmental law**). The units proceed from general legal topics to more specific.

The left-hand page of each unit presents **legal terms and expressions in context** and the right-hand page is designed to let you check and develop your understanding of them and how they are used through a series of exercises. Key terms or expressions may occur in more than one unit.

There is an **answer key** at the back of the book. Most of the exercises have questions with only one correct answer. If there is more than one possible answer the exercise tells you. Some of the exercises, including the **Over to you** activities at the end of each unit (see below), are designed for discussion and/or writing about the legal jurisdiction you work or study in.

Where appropriate, **website addresses** at the bottom of the right-hand pages give links to further information in English on related legal topics.

Also at the end of the book there is an **index** which lists the key words and phrases which have been highlighted and gives the unit numbers in which they appear. The index also tells you how the words and expressions are pronounced.

The left-hand page

The texts on the left-hand page vary in length. Each text has a clear heading. Some texts are from spoken contexts; others from written. Some are from formal contexts, for example an extract from legislation, or contract terms, or a formal presentation; others are from more informal interactions, for example discussions between legal colleagues talking about aspects of their work. Some units draw your attention to characteristic features of legal language in English or to differences between legal English usage in the United States and England. All the units highlight typical word combinations.

The right-hand page

A range of exercises on the right-hand page give practice in using the highlighted legal vocabulary and expressions from the left-hand page. Sometimes the exercises provide practice in contexts like emails between legal colleagues, letters to clients, contract terms, or legal forms. Other exercises focus on checking comprehension of meaning or distinctions in use between similar words, stress in pronunciation, or the formation of words.

'Over to you' activities

These activities give you the chance to practise using English legal language to write or talk about aspects of a legal jurisdiction known to you, and about your own work, study, or opinions. Self-study learners can do these as a written activity or set up a computer blog to share ideas with others wanting to develop their legal English vocabulary through practice.

In the classroom, the **Over to you** activities can be used as the basis for discussion in small groups, with a spokesperson for each group summarising the discussion and its outcome for the class. Alternatively, pairs can exchange views, ideas, or information and then combine with another pair to report on their discussion. The teacher can monitor the discussions for appropriate and accurate use of vocabulary. Learners can follow up by using the **Over to you** as a written activity, for example for homework. Learners might do more research on language use by exploring the suggested **web links**.

How to use the book for self-study

Find a topic you are looking for by referring to the contents page or the index. Quickly write in note form in English what you already know about the topic and any questions you have. Then read through the texts on the left-hand page of the unit. If you are unsure of the meaning of terms, try to guess the meaning from the context as you read. Do the exercises on the right-hand page. Check your answers in the key. If you have made any mistakes look at the text again and check the exercise. Write down useful words in a notebook; notice how they are used in other texts. If you are still unsure of any words, look them up in a law dictionary. There are also legal glossaries online.

How to use the book in the classroom

Teachers can choose the units that relate to learners' particular needs and interests, or themes which the course is focusing on. Learners can work on the units in pairs or individually, the teacher going round the class listening and advising. Teachers should encourage learners to discuss why one answer is possible and others are not.

We hope you find the book useful and easy to use. We would welcome your comments and suggestions on using it.

1 Legal systems

A The structure of the law

The legal system in the United Kingdom (UK)

The study of law distinguishes between **public law** and **private law**, but in legal practice in the UK the distinction between **civil law** and **criminal law** is more important to practising lawyers. Public law relates to the state. It is concerned with laws which govern processes in local and national government and **conflicts between** the individual and the state in areas such as immigration and social security. Private law is concerned with the relationships between **legal persons**, that is, individuals and corporations, and includes family law, contract law and property law. Criminal law deals with certain forms of **conduct** for which the state **reserves punishment**, for example murder and theft. The **state prosecutes the offender**. Civil law concerns relationships between private persons, their rights, and their duties. It is also concerned with conduct which may **give rise to a claim** by a legal person **for compensation** or an **injunction** – an order made by the court. However, each field of law tends to overlap with others. For example, a road accident case may lead to a criminal prosecution as well as a civil action for compensation.

Substantive law creates, defines or **regulates rights**, **liabilities**, and **duties** in all areas of law and is contrasted with **procedural law**, which defines the procedure by which a **law** is to be **enforced**.

B The constitution

The **head of state** is the monarch, currently the Queen in the UK, but the government carries the authority of the Crown (the monarch). The Westminster Parliament has two **chambers**: the House of Lords and the House of Commons, which **sit separately** and are **constituted on** different principles. The Commons is an **elected body** of members. Substantial reform is being carried out in the **upper house**, the House of Lords, where it is proposed that the majority of members be **appointed**, with a minority **elected**, replacing the hereditary peers. There is no **written constitution**, but **constitutional law** consists of **statute law** (see Unit 2), **common law** (see Unit 3), and **constitutional conventions**.

C Jurisdiction

There are four countries and three distinct **jurisdictions** in the United Kingdom: England and Wales, Scotland, and Northern Ireland. All share a **legislature** in the Westminster Parliament for the making of new laws and have a common law tradition, but each has its own **hierarchy of courts**, legal rules and legal profession. Wales and Northern Ireland each have their own **Assembly** and since 1999 Scottish **Members of Parliament** (SMPs) have sat in their own Parliament. **Under an Act** of the Westminster Parliament, the Scottish Parliament has power to **legislate** on any subject not specifically **reserved to** the Westminster Parliament such as defence or foreign policy. The UK's **accession to** the European Communities in 1973, **authorised by** the European Communities Act 1972, has meant the addition of a further **legislative authority** in the legal system. The UK is also a **signatory of** the European **Convention** of Human Rights and this has been **incorporated into** UK law.

1.1 Complete the definitions. Look at A opposite to help you.

1 .... is law relating to acts committed against the law which are punished by the state.

2 .... is concerned with the constitution or government of the state, or the relationship between state and citizens.

3 .... is rules which determine how a case is administered by the courts.

4 .... is concerned with the rights and duties of individuals, organisations, and associations (such as companies, trade unions, and charities), as opposed to criminal law.

5 .... is common law and statute law used by the courts in making decisions.

1.2 Complete the sentences. Look at B and C opposite to help you. There is more than one possibility for one of the answers.

1 In many systems a president rather than a monarch is ....
....

2 The UK system has a parliament with two ....

3 As in other countries, the courts are organised in a .... of levels.

4 The Scottish Parliament has the .... to legislate on subjects not reserved to Westminster.

5 The EC is an important legislative .... in most European countries.

6 A number of international .... have been incorporated into national law.

1.3 Complete the table with words from A, B and C opposite and related forms. Put a stress mark in front of the stressed syllable in each word. The first one has been done for you. Then complete the sentences below with words from the table.

Verb	Noun	Adjective
'constitute	consti'tution	consti'tutional
legislate		
proceed		
convene		
	regulation	
accede		
elect		
authorise		

1 The .... is the body which has the function of making law; normally it is the Parliament.

2 It is quite a lengthy process to .... to the European Community.

3 Sometimes a court case can be delayed while counsel argue over .... problems.

Over to you

Describe some of the distinctive features of your legal system and constitution, first as if to a foreign lawyer, then as if to a foreign lay person.

For more information on the UK Parliament and legislative processes, go to: www.parliament.uk; for the US Senate, go to: www.senate.gov/.

2 Sources of law: legislation

A Background to making new law

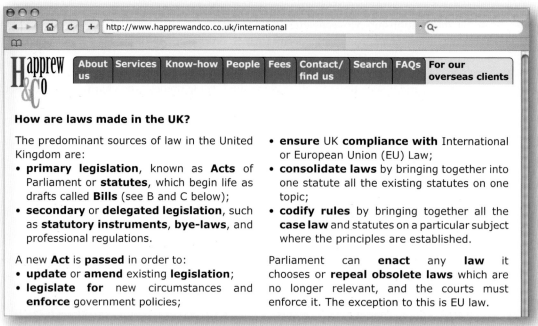

How are laws made in the UK?

The predominant sources of law in the United Kingdom are:
- **primary legislation**, known as **Acts** of Parliament or **statutes**, which begin life as drafts called **Bills** (see B and C below);
- **secondary** or **delegated legislation**, such as **statutory instruments**, **bye-laws**, and professional regulations.

A new **Act** is **passed** in order to:
- **update** or **amend** existing **legislation**;
- **legislate for** new circumstances and **enforce** government policies;
- **ensure** UK **compliance with** International or European Union (EU) Law;
- **consolidate laws** by bringing together into one statute all the existing statutes on one topic;
- **codify rules** by bringing together all the **case law** and statutes on a particular subject where the principles are established.

Parliament can **enact** any **law** it chooses or **repeal obsolete laws** which are no longer relevant, and the courts must enforce it. The exception to this is EU law.

Note: **Act** of Parliament and **Bill** are always capitalised in legal usage; **statute** is not.
Statutory instruments are delegated legislation created by government ministers.
Bye-laws are made by Local Government or public bodies.

BrE: an Act; AmE: a Bill

B Early development of a Bill

The government may proceed to **initiate a consultative process** by the publication of a Green Paper in which its **proposals** are **set out** at an early stage with the intention of attracting public response and comment. The government's White Papers contain their more definite proposals, although these are often published following consultation or discussion with **pressure groups**, **professional bodies**, or **voluntary organisations**. A Bill does not have to be preceded by a White or Green paper, although it may have been presented for **public scrutiny**, that is, examination, in draft form earlier.

C Passing an Act

All Acts must be **submitted to** both Houses of Parliament in the draft form of a Bill. The legislative process involves three **readings** in both Houses. At the first reading, the title is read to Members of Parliament (MPs); at the second reading, MPs **debate** proposals. Then a standing committee will **scrutinise the provisions** in the Bill and may amend it to ensure that it **enshrines the principles** debated and **approved** at the second reading. This is reported back to MPs. At the third reading, the Bill is **re-presented**. The Bill then goes through readings in the upper house. The actual drafting of the legislation is **undertaken** by Parliamentary Counsel. Finally, a Bill must receive Royal Assent from the monarch before it **becomes law** on a specified date. In fact, this stage has been reduced to a formal reading of the short title of an Act in both Houses of Parliament and is now a formality.

Government Bills are **introduced** by the Government; **Private Members Bills** are **proposed** by MPs. Both methods may result in **Public Acts** that govern the general public. **Private Acts** affect particular individuals or institutions.

Note: No article (a/the) is necessary in **to become law**.

2.1 Find verbs in A opposite that can be used to make word combinations with the words below. There is more than one possibility for three of the answers.

Parliament can

1 .... Acts of Parliament.
2 .... new statutes.
3 .... existing legislation.
4 .... obsolete law.
5 .... statute law, case law, and amendments into one Act.
6 .... law by repealing and re-enacting in one statute provisions of a number of statutes on the same subject.

2.2 Complete the sentences. Look at A, B and C opposite to help you. Pay attention to the grammatical context.

1 An order made under authority delegated to a government minister by an Act of Parliament is known as a ....
....

2 A .... is made by a local authority or a public or nationalised body and has to be approved by central government.

3 Charities like Oxfam and Help the Aged can act as ....
.... , lobbying for law reform.

4 The Committee needs to ensure the Bill incorporates the principles agreed so they check it by ....
....

Freedom of Information Act 2000

CHAPTER 36

An Act of Parliament

2.3 A visiting Russian colleague is asking an English solicitor about the legislative process. Replace the underlined words in their conversation with alternative words from C opposite. Pay attention to the grammatical context. There is more than one possibility for two of the answers.

Natasha: How is new legislation enacted?
Charles: Well, initially the (1) draft legislation has to be (2) presented to both houses. The draft is (3) discussed several times. A committee has the job of checking that the Bill (4) incorporates the fundamental elements (5) agreed at the second reading. After this, the Bill is (6) shown again to the lower house.
Natasha: Who does the (7) formal writing of the legislation?
Charles: It's (8) done by qualified barristers employed as civil servants, known as Parliamentary Counsel.
Natasha: Who can (9) put forward Bills?
Charles: The government and, less commonly, MPs.

Over to you

Describe the process of making new law in your country. What are the strengths and weaknesses of the process?

For more information on the UK Parliament and legislative processes, go to: www.parliament.uk. For legislation around the world, go to: www.lexadin.nl/wlg/legis/nofr/legis.htm

3 Sources of law: common law

A Common law in the UK

Penny Arkwright **practises** in the High Court. She is speaking at an international convention for young lawyers.

'The legal system in many countries, including Australia, Canada (except Quebec), Ghana, Hong Kong, India, Jamaica, Malaysia, New Zealand, Pakistan, Tanzania, the USA (except Louisiana), the Bahamas, and Zambia, is based on **common law**. The common law consists of the substantive law and procedural rules that are created by the **judicial decisions** made in the courts. Although legislation may **override** such decisions, the legislation itself is **subject to interpretation** and refinement in the courts.

Essential to the common law is the **hierarchy of the courts** in all of the UK jurisdictions and the **principle of binding precedent**. In practice, this means that the decision of a higher court is **binding on** a lower court, that is, the decision must be followed, and in the course of a trial the judges must refer to existing precedents. They'll also **consider** decisions made in a lower court, although they're not **bound to follow** them. However, a rule set by a court of greater or equal status must be **applied** if it's **to the point** – relevant or pertinent.

During a trial, **counsel** will **cite cases** and either attempt to **distinguish the case** at trial **from** those **referred to** or, alternatively, argue that **the rule at law reasoned** and established in a previous case is **applicable** and should be followed. Hence the term **case law**. A case will inevitably involve many facts and issues of evidence. The eventual decision itself doesn't actually **set the precedent**. The precedent is the rule of law which the first instance judge **relied on** in determining the case's outcome.

Judges in a case may make other **statements of law**. Whilst not constituting binding precedents, these may be considered in subsequent cases and may be cited as **persuasive authority**, if appropriate. Since the Human Rights Act of 1988, all courts in the United Kingdom must now refer to the ultimate authority of the European Court of Human Rights, including all previous decisions made by that court.'

Note: **practises** – qualified to work professionally

B Law reports

'The development and **application of the common law system** pivots upon the existence of a comprehensive system of reporting cases. The Law Reports, published annually by the Council of Law Reporting, are perhaps the most authoritative and frequently cited set of reports, differing from other **series of law reports**, such as Butterworth's All England Law Reports [All ER] or specialist reports like Lloyds Law Reports, in that they contain summaries of counsel's arguments and are **revised** by the judge sitting in each respective case before publication. Cases aren't always reported in the year that they are decided so a **case citation** will refer to the volume and year in which the case was published, for example *Meah v Roberts*, [1978] 1 All ER 97. Developments in electronic databases have increased public access to recent cases.'

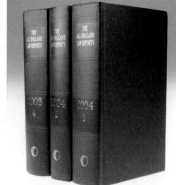

Note: Latin terms used for the legal principles outlined in the above texts are:
stare decisis – **principles of binding precedent**
ratio decidendi – **the rule at law reasoned**
obiter dictum – **persuasive authority**
In a civil case citation, for example *Meah v Roberts,* [1978] 1 All ER 97, **v** (Latin for *versus*) is said **'and'.**

Butterworth's All England Law Reports

3.1 Penny Arkwright is talking about her experience of court cases to a Russian colleague. Replace the underlined words and phrases with alternative words and phrases from A and B opposite. Pay attention to the grammatical context. There is more than one possibility for one of the answers.

1 The courts are <u>compelled</u> to apply the precedent set by a higher court.

2 During the court case the judge will <u>evaluate</u> all the evidence and the legal issues.

3 Judges are required to <u>follow</u> the ratio, or reasoning, in relevant previous decided cases.

4 However, the judge may <u>note</u> a case cited as precedent by counsel as materially different from the one at trial.

5 It is, however, the role of counsel to <u>refer to</u> relevant previous case decisions.

6 The principle of <u>following the decisions of higher courts</u> is fundamental to case law.

7 The Law Reports series are the most frequently cited reports because the text is <u>edited</u> by the trial judge.

8 New legislation may <u>pay no attention to</u> the decision of an earlier court judgment.

3.2 Complete the table with words from A and B opposite and related forms. Put a stress mark in front of the stressed syllable in each word. The first one has been done for you.

Verb	Noun	Adjective
'cite	ci'tation	
apply		
precede		
	persuasion	
bind		

3.3 Penny is working with a trainee barrister. Complete her sentences with appropriate words from the table above.

1 Well, that decision of the Appeal Court is going to be .... on the case we've got at trial just now.

2 We need to be able to convince the judge that the rule in *Meah v Roberts* is .... to this case.

3 Can you check the case .... ? I think the year's wrong.

4 Should we add to our argument that *Edwards v Peck* is a .... precedent given the legal issues, although the judge isn't bound to follow it?

Over to you

Explain to a colleague from a different jurisdiction how cases are used and recorded in your legal system.

To look at some recent UK case reports, go to: www.courtservice.gov.uk and www.lawreports.co.uk/.

4 The court system

A Civil courts

Duncan Ritchie, a barrister, is talking to a visiting group of young European lawyers.

'Both criminal and civil courts in England and Wales primarily **hear evidence** and aim to determine what exactly happened in a case. Broadly speaking, the lower courts decide **matters of fact** and the upper courts normally deal with **points of law**. In England, simple **civil actions**, for example family matters such as undefended divorce, are normally heard in either the **Magistrates' Courts** or the **County Courts**.

Judges have different titles depending on their experience, training, and level. A single **stipendiary magistrate** or three **lay magistrates** sit in the Magistrates' Court. There's no **jury** in a Magistrates' Court. Family cases may **go on appeal from** the Magistrates' Court **to** the County Courts. The County Court also hears complex **first instance** civil cases, such as contract disputes, compensation claims, consumer complaints about faulty goods or services, and bankruptcy cases. **Claimants**, previously referred to as **plaintiffs**, may **seek a legal remedy** for some **harm or injury** they have **suffered**. There are **circuit judges** and **recorders** who sit in the County Courts, usually without a jury. Juries are now rare in civil actions, so normally the judge considers both law and fact.

More complex civil cases, such as the administration of estates and actions for the recovery of land, are heard in **the High Court of Justice**, which is divided into three **divisions**: Family, Chancery and Queen's Bench. The court has both **original**, that is, first instance, and **appellate jurisdiction**. From the High Court cases may go on appeal to the civil division of **the Court of Appeal**, which can **reverse** or **uphold a decision** of the lower courts. Its decisions bind all the lower civil courts. Civil cases may **leapfrog** from the High Court to **the House of Lords**, bypassing the Court of Appeal, when points of law of general public importance are involved. **Appellants** must, however, **apply for leave to appeal**. Decisions of the House of Lords are binding on all other courts but not necessarily on itself. The court of the House of Lords consists of twelve life peers appointed from judges and barristers. The **quorum**, or minimum number, of law lords for an **appeal hearing** is normally three, but generally there is a **sitting** of five judges.'

Note: A **stipendiary** is a full-time paid magistrate who has qualified as a lawyer.
A **lay magistrate** is unpaid and is an established member of the local community.
A **circuit** is a geographical division for legal purposes; England and Wales are divided into six.
A **recorder** is a part-time judge with ten years standing as a barrister or solicitor.
See Unit 12 for more information about judges. See B below for more information about juries.

B Criminal courts

'About 95% of all criminal cases in England and Wales are tried in the Magistrates' Courts, which deal with **petty crimes**, that is, less serious ones. In certain circumstances, the court may commit an accused person to **the Crown Court** for more severe punishment, either by way of a **fine** or **imprisonment**. Except in cases of homicide, children under 14 and young persons – that is, **minors** between 14 and 17 years of age – must always be **tried summarily**, meaning without a jury, by a Youth Court. A Youth Court is a branch of the Magistrates' Court. **Indictable offences**, that is, more serious ones such as theft, assault, drug dealing, and murder, are **reserved for trial** in the Crown Court. In almost all criminal cases, the State, in the name of the Crown, **prosecutes** a person **alleged to have committed** a crime. In England and Wales, a jury of twelve people decides whether the defendant is guilty of the crime she or he is **charged with**. The Crown Court may hear cases in circuit areas. From the Crown Court, **appeal against conviction or sentence** lies to the Criminal Division of the Court of Appeal. If **leave to appeal** is **granted** by that court, cases may go on appeal to the House of Lords.'

4.1 Complete the diagram. Look at A and B opposite to help you.

The Court System in England and Wales

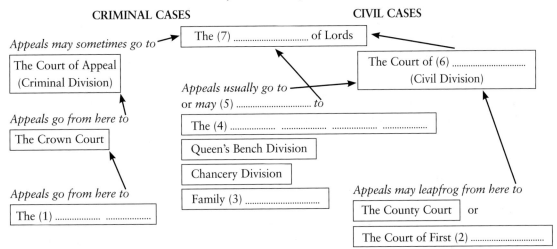

CRIMINAL CASES   CIVIL CASES

Appeals may sometimes go to → The (7) .... of Lords ←

The Court of Appeal
(Criminal Division)

The Court of (6) ....
(Civil Division)

Appeals usually go to
or may (5) .... to

Appeals go from here to

The Crown Court

The (4) ....

Queen's Bench Division

Chancery Division

Appeals go from here to

Family (3) ....

The (1) ....

Appeals may leapfrog from here to

The County Court   or

The Court of First (2) ....

4.2 Complete the table with words from A and B opposite and related forms. Put a stress mark in front of the stressed syllable in each word. The first one has been done for you.

Verb	Noun – event or action	Noun – person
'sit	'sitting	
appeal		
hear		
try		
claim		

4.3 Match the two parts of the sentences and complete the gaps with words from the table above. Pay attention to the grammatical context. There is more than one possibility for three of the gaps.

1 The .... courts can
2 An appellant must get
3 In a civil action, a .... who has suffered
4 Magistrates generally .... cases of petty crime as
5 Indictable offences are

a a court of first instance.
b normally .... in the Crown Court.
c reverse or uphold decisions of lower courts.
d harm or injury seeks a remedy.
e leave to .... before taking a case to a higher court.

Over to you

Draw a diagram of your court system and explain the court structure as if to a foreign client who is pursuing an action in your courts. Use your own language for the names of the courts but use English to describe their function.

For more information on UK courts, go to: www.courtservice.gov.uk; for other courts, go to: www.lexadin.nl/wlg/courts/nofr/courts.htm

5 Criminal justice and criminal proceedings

Duncan Ritchie, a barrister, is talking to a visiting group of young European lawyers.

A Criminal justice

'The state **prosecutes** those **charged with a crime**. The police **investigate a crime** and may **apprehend suspects** and **detain them in custody**. If the police decide an **offender** should be prosecuted, a file on the case is sent to the Crown Prosecution Service (CPS) – the national prosecution service for England and Wales. The CPS must consider whether there is enough **evidence** for a **realistic prospect of conviction**, and if so, whether the public interest requires a prosecution. They can decide to either go ahead with the prosecution, send the case back to the police for a **caution**, or take no further action. **Criminal proceedings** can be **initiated** either by **the serving of a summons** setting out the offence and requiring **the accused** to attend court, or, in more serious cases, by a **warrant of arrest** issued by a Magistrates' Court. Lawyers from the CPS may act as **public prosecutors**. The Criminal Defence Service provides **legal aid**, which funds the services of an independent duty solicitor who represents the accused in the police station and in court. However, at the end of a Crown Court case the judge has the power to order the defendant to pay some or all of the **defence costs**.'

Note: If Green is prosecuted for a crime, the ensuing trial will be called the case of **R v** Green. **R** is the abbreviation for the Crown (*Regina* for a Queen or *Rex* for a King); **v** (Latin for *versus*) is said **'against'** in a criminal case.

B Categories of criminal offence

'There are three categories of criminal offence. **Summary offences**, tried without a jury, are minor crimes only **triable** in the Magistrates' Court. **Indictable offences** are serious crimes, such as murder, which can only be heard in the Crown Court. The formal document containing the **alleged offences**, supported by facts, is called the **indictment**. A case which can be heard in either the Magistrates' Court or the Crown Court, such as theft or burglary, is **triable either way**. If the defendant **pleads guilty**, the Magistrates' Court can either **proceed to sentence** or **commit to the Crown Court for sentence**, where more **severe penalties** are available. If there is a **not guilty plea**, the court can decide the mode of trial. The person charged may request a **trial by jury**. If granted, such trials take place in the Crown Court.'

Note: indictable offences are also known as **notifiable offences** in the UK.

C Criminal court proceedings

'The English system of justice is **adversarial**, which means that each side collects and presents their own evidence and attacks their opponent's by **cross-examination**. In a criminal trial, **the burden of proof is on** the prosecution to **prove beyond reasonable doubt** that the accused is guilty. A **person accused** or **under arrest** for an offence may be **granted bail** and temporarily released. However, bail may be refused, for example if there are **grounds for believing** that the accused would **fail to appear for trial** or commit an offence. In the Crown Court, there may be a **preparatory hearing** for a complex case before the **jury** is **sworn in**. Prior to the trial, there is a statutory requirement for **disclosure** by the prosecution and defence of material relevant to the case, for example details of any **alibis** – people who can provide proof of the accused's whereabouts at the time of the crime – or **witnesses** – people who may have seen something relevent to the crime. Once a trial has begun, the defendant may be advised by counsel to change his or her plea to guilty, in expectation of a **reduced sentence**. If, at the end of the trial, the court's **verdict** is not guilty, then the defendant is **acquitted**.'

5.1 Complete the definitions. Look at A and B opposite to help you.

1 a .... – a court document authorising the police to detain someone

2 an .... – a written statement with details of the crimes someone is charged with

3 a .... – a formal order to attend court

5.2 Make word combinations from A, B and C opposite using words from the box. Then use appropriate word combinations to complete the sentences below.

criminal	doubt	sentence	indictable	severe	plea	realistic	guilty
reasonable	defence	proceedings	costs		reduced	prospect	offences	penalties

1 The Crown Prosecutor considers whether there's sufficient evidence to provide a ....
.... of conviction.

2 There should be no conviction without proof beyond ....

3 The Crown Court always hears .... such as manslaughter.

4 In sentencing serious crimes, courts can impose ....

5 At the end of a trial, a defendant may be ordered to pay a contribution towards ....
....

5.3 Replace the underlined words and phrases with alternative words and phrases from A, B and C opposite. Pay attention to the grammatical context. There is more than one possibility for one of the answers.

a Bail may be refused and the defendant may be (1) held in police custody.

b Alternatively, the defendant may be (2) found not guilty by the court and discharged.

c Once proceedings have been initiated, the defendant (3) comes before the court.

d The police formally (4) accuse the suspect in the police station.

e If the offender pleads guilty in the Magistrates' Court, the court imposes a (5) punishment.

f The police investigate a serious offence and (6) arrest a suspect.

g The suspect may ask for (7) release from custody before the trial.

5.4 Put the sentences in 5.3 into the correct order chronologically. Look at A, B and C opposite to help you. The first stage is f.

Over to you

Describe the process of a criminal trial in your legal system as if to a client from a different system.

For more information on the UK Crown Prosecution Service, go to: www.cps.gov.uk/; for the US Department of Justice, go to: www.usdoj.gov/.

6 Civil procedure

A Civil Procedure Rules

Alisdair Hannah, a barrister, is talking to a visiting group of young European lawyers.

'All cases concerning goods, property, **debt repayment**, **breach of contract** (with some exceptions such as **insolvency proceedings** and **non-contentious litigation**), are subject to Civil Procedure Rules. The Rules, which **came into force** in 1999 in England and Wales, made radical changes to civil process in the County Court and the High Court.

The judge performs the role of case manager. The court **sets a timetable** for litigation, with the parties being under an obligation to the court to **adhere to timescales** which control the progress of the case. Procedure rules are **supplemented** by detailed instructions made by the judge which support the rules, known as **practice directions**.'

B Proceeding with a claim

'Most **claims** are **initiated** by the use of a **claim form**, which functions as a **summons**. The claim form can be used for different types of claim, for example for **specified** or **unspecified monetary sums**, or for the **claimant** to ask the court to **make an order**. Once a claim has been **issued**, a copy is **served on**, that is, delivered to, the **defendant** with a response pack inviting them to either **admit the claim**, using a **form of admission**, or to defend it, using a **form of defence**. The response pack also contains an **acknowledgement of service** form to confirm receipt of the claim, and a **counterclaim** form for the defendant to use if they wish to claim against the claimant. A defendant must respond within 14 days of service of the **particulars** of the claim. If the defendant does not respond, **judgment** may be **given in favour of the claimant**. The defendant may be able to **get a time extension** for **filing a reply** on defence by using the part of the acknowledgement of service form which states an intention to defend the claim.

Cases are **allocated to a regime** or **track** by a **procedural judge** according to their **monetary value**. Claims of £5,000 or less are allocated to a **small claims** track while claims of up to £15,000 are allocated to a **fast track**. More complex claims with a greater value are allocated to a **multi track** regime. Fast track directions might include **disclosure**, where the claimant tells the defence of any relevant documents in their possession. This is followed by **inspection**, initiated by a written request by the claimant to look at relevant documents held by the defence, and an exchange of **witness statements**. The multi track regime is intended to be flexible and does not have a standard procedure. In all regimes, parties are encouraged to **settle their differences** and for this purpose a **stay in proceedings**, that is, a temporary halt, may be **agreed**. **Case management conferences** are often conducted by telephone and give parties the opportunity to **review the process** and make decisions. If a defendant is ordered to pay by a judge and fails to do so, the claimant can **enforce the judgment** in the Magistrates' Court.'

Note: The reforms to the Civil Procedure Rules led by Woolf in 1998 included the following changes in legal language:
claim form, formerly known as a **writ of summons**
specified, formerly known as a **liquidated** claim (a fixed monetary sum)
claimant, formerly known as a **plaintiff**

6.1 Complete the definitions. Look at A and B opposite to help you.

1 .... – the process by which a claimant may look at written evidence held by the defence

2 .... – the document in which the defendant makes a claim against the claimant

3 .... – the document in which the defendant agrees to the claim made by the claimant

4 .... – the document starting a claim proceedings

5 .... – the process by which the claimant is required to inform the defendant of documents they hold relevant to the claim

6 .... – the document giving evidence by someone who saw or heard something critical to the case

7 .... – the instructions given by a judge on how procedures should be carried out in a case

6.2 Make word combinations from A and B opposite using a word from each box. Then use appropriate word combinations and information in B opposite to answer the questions below.

admit	a timetable
agree to	a stay
allocate to	a claim
enforce	the process
file	the judgment
issue	a claim
review	a claim on
serve	a regime
set	differences
settle	a reply

1 How does a claim proceeding start?

....

2 What must a defendant do when he or she has been served with a claim?

....

3 If both parties want time to try to settle the dispute out of court, what should they ask the court to do?

....

4 What is the purpose of a case management conference?

....

5 If a defendant is ordered to pay a claimant's costs but does not, what action can the claimant take?

....

A solicitor discusses a claim.

Over to you

Describe the process of a civil claim in your legal system as if to a client from a different system who wants to initiate a claim. Use an example if possible.

For more information on civil procedure in England and Wales, go to: www.hmcourts-service.gov.uk; for Scottish civil procedure, go to: www.scotcourts.gov.uk/

7 Tribunals

A The status and range of tribunals

Tribunals in the UK

The system of courts in the United Kingdom is supplemented by a substantial number of **tribunals**, set up by Acts of Parliament. They are described in the guidance given to government departments as:

"those **bodies** whose functions, like those of courts of law, are essentially **judicial**. Independently of **the Executive**, they decide the rights and obligations of private citizens towards each other and towards a government department or public authority."
Report of Council on Tribunals

The growth in the number and importance of tribunals is closely related to the development of an increasingly active welfare state with legislation covering areas previously considered private. Some examples are:

- Social Security Appeal Tribunal
- Employment Tribunal
- Mental Health Review Tribunal
- Immigration Appeal Tribunal
- Lands Tribunal

Some tribunals have a significant effect in the areas of law involved. However, they are nonetheless inferior to the courts and their decisions are **subject to judicial review** – examination by a higher court of the decision-making process in a lower court.

B Composition of tribunals and procedure

A tribunal consists of three members. The **chairperson** is normally the only legally qualified member. The other two are **lay representatives** who usually have **special expertise** in the area governed by the tribunal, gained from practical experience. The tribunal will also have all the usual administrative support enjoyed by a court: hearing clerks, who are responsible for administering procedures, clerical staff, and hearing accommodation.

The intention of tribunals was to provide a less formal proceeding in which **claimants** could **lodge claims** and **respondents defend claims**, and ultimately **resolve** their **disputes** without the need for legal representation. However, procedures have become more complicated and cases **brought before** tribunals are often presented by solicitors and barristers. For example, a case of **unfair dismissal** – where an employer appears to not be acting in a reasonable way in removing an employee – could be brought to an Employment Tribunal. Procedure at that Tribunal may include a stage where a **government agency** tries to **broker a settlement** so that a **claim may be withdrawn**. The costs of the hearing are **borne by the public purse**, that is, paid from tax revenue, but legal representation is at the cost of each party. **Witness statements** are normally exchanged before the hearing and at the hearing both **parties** may question witnesses and **address the Tribunal**. The Tribunal can **refer to decisions of higher courts** before making its decision in a specific case.

A tribunal in action

7.1 Complete this letter which a lawyer has written to his client about a case coming to an Employment Tribunal. Look at B opposite to help you.

Woods & Pankhurst Solicitors

3 The Old Forge
West Cambourne
Cambs
CB6 7AB

Mr D Johnson,
Managing Director, Force Ltd

Dear David,

Claim for Unfair Dismissal by A.J. Blackwood

Many thanks for your faxed letter of yesterday attaching the copy ET1 in respect of the above. According to my records, Force Ltd have not had an (1) .... claim made against it previously so I thought it would be helpful if I gave you a brief outline of the various stages of the procedure involved for you to (2) .... the claim.

Following receipt of the ET1, the company, as (3) .... , has 28 days to complete and return a defence on form ET3. The Tribunal will acknowledge receipt of this and will forward a copy to Miss Blackwood, the (4) ....

The Tribunal appoints an officer of the (5) .... , the Arbitration Conciliation and Advisory Service (ACAS), to this case. He or she will get in touch with both you and Miss Blackwood for the purpose of offering assistance to broker a Settlement Agreement so that the claim can be (6) .... Obviously, if this is possible then the costs of a Tribunal hearing will be saved. The costs of a hearing are (7) .... the public purse, although obviously you will be responsible for this firm's fees in representing you if required.

Usually the Tribunal allows ACAS a number of weeks in which to (8) .... If that doesn't happen, a date for the case to be heard will be arranged. When that date has been determined, the Tribunal will give both (9) .... a simple set of directions to prepare for the hearing. I would normally expect to agree a bundle of relevant documents with the other side and to exchange written witness statements in advance of the hearing.

At the hearing, witnesses will be asked to swear or affirm that the contents of their (10) .... are true. Both parties and the Tribunal will have the chance to question the witnesses. Following that, Miss Blackwood and you on behalf of the company (or your respective legal representatives) may (11) .... the Tribunal with an argument about why your evidence and case should be accepted. The Tribunal may also consider points about the relevant law at this point and possibly (12) .... decisions made at a higher level of the Tribunal system, such as the Employment Appeal Tribunal, the Court of Appeal, the House of Lords, or even the European Court of Justice, before reaching its decision.

I hope this is helpful to you. Obviously, we will need to discuss in some detail the facts of the matter and the merit, or otherwise, of the claim when we meet on Friday. I already have a copy of Miss Blackwood's contract so will make sure I have that to hand. I look forward to seeing you then.

Kind regards.

Yours sincerely,

Paul Hedges

Paul Hedges
Partner, Woods & Pankhurst

Over to you

Describe how disputes between private citizens are resolved in your legal system. What are some of the advantages and disadvantages of tribunals?

For information on UK tribunals, go to: www.council-on-tribunals.gov.uk/.

8 European Union law

A What is the EU?

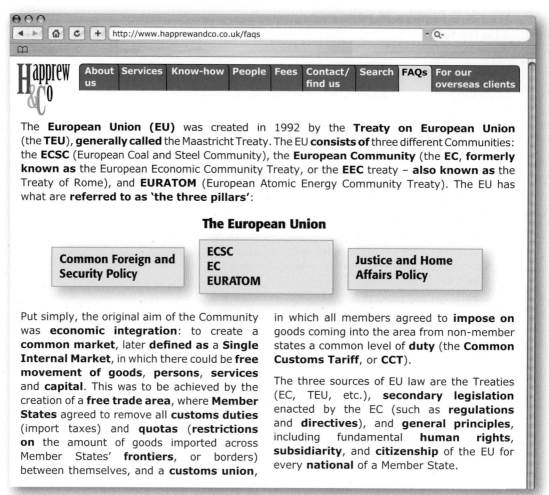

http://www.happrewandco.co.uk/faqs

Happrew &Co

| About us | Services | Know-how | People | Fees | Contact/ find us | Search | FAQs | For our overseas clients |

The **European Union (EU)** was created in 1992 by the **Treaty on European Union** (the **TEU**), **generally called** the Maastricht Treaty. The EU **consists of** three different Communities: the **ECSC** (European Coal and Steel Community), the **European Community** (the **EC, formerly known as** the European Economic Community Treaty, or the **EEC** treaty – **also known as** the Treaty of Rome), and **EURATOM** (European Atomic Energy Community Treaty). The EU has what are **referred to as 'the three pillars'**:

The European Union

| Common Foreign and Security Policy | ECSC EC EURATOM | Justice and Home Affairs Policy |

Put simply, the original aim of the Community was **economic integration**: to create a **common market**, later **defined as** a **Single Internal Market**, in which there could be **free movement of goods**, **persons**, **services** and **capital**. This was to be achieved by the creation of a **free trade area**, where **Member States** agreed to remove all **customs duties** (import taxes) and **quotas** (**restrictions on** the amount of goods imported across Member States' **frontiers**, or borders) between themselves, and a **customs union**, in which all members agreed to **impose on** goods coming into the area from non-member states a common level of **duty** (the **Common Customs Tariff**, or **CCT**).

The three sources of EU law are the Treaties (EC, TEU, etc.), **secondary legislation** enacted by the EC (such as **regulations** and **directives**), and **general principles**, including fundamental **human rights**, **subsidiarity**, and **citizenship** of the EU for every **national** of a Member State.

Note: subsidiarity – the Community may only take legal action where it **has exclusive competence**, that is, power to govern, and where an action cannot be achieved by member states acting within their natural institutions, for example a trans-national action.

B How does the EU impact on Member States?

The EC Treaty is **directly applicable in** every Member State. **Accession to** (membership of) the Community limits the power of national governments and affects **national sovereignty** – the power to govern. Community law **has supremacy over**, that is, overrides, national law. This supremacy was established in the case of Costa v ENEL (Case 6/64) ECR 545. The **Single European Act 1986** made **provisions** (legal conditions) creating an **obligation on** the Community to **take** the necessary **measures** to achieve the Internal Market. Under Article 249 (ex Art 189) there are five types of legal act which the Community may use:

- **Regulations** – have **general application** and are **binding in their entirety on** all Member States and **have direct effect**, meaning they automatically become law in Member States.
- **Directives** – are binding on Member States as to their result but do not bind individuals until they have been **transposed into national law** (implemented).
- **Decisions** of the **European Court of Justice (ECJ)** – are binding on those to whom they are addressed.
- **Recommendations** and **opinions** – have **no binding force** but may be **persuasive**, that is, have influence.

8.1 Find five phrases in A opposite used to indicate that a term has another name, for example 'formerly known as'. Then use appropriate phrases to complete the sentences below. There is more than one possibility for one of the answers.

1 Under EC law, anything which can be bought or sold is .... goods.
2 Beijing was .... Peking in the West.
3 Customs duty is .... any charge that is imposed on goods because they are imported.
4 The third pillar of the European Union, ... the Justice and Home Affairs pillar, is incorporated into the EC treaty.

8.2 Rearrange the underlined letters to make words in the extracts below. Look at A and B opposite to help you.

> The (1) <u>laennirt</u> market shall comprise an area without internal (2) <u>stenroirf</u> in which the (3) <u>reef</u> (4) <u>vemmnote</u> of goods, persons, (5) <u>essricev</u> and capital is ensured in accordance with the (6) <u>noopssivir</u> of this (7) <u>yetrat</u>.
>
> *from Article 7a, the Single European Act 1986*

> Member (8) <u>eattss</u> shall take all appropriate (9) <u>russeame</u> whether general or particular, to ensure fulfilment of the (10) <u>tooglisnabi</u> arising out of this Treaty or resulting from an action taken by the institutions of the (11) <u>timmouncy</u>. They shall facilitate achievement of the Community's tasks.
>
> *from Article 5, the EC Treaty*

> A (12) <u>ulegnotair</u> shall have general (13) <u>pintclapoia</u>. It shall be binding in its (14) <u>teentryi</u> and directly (15) <u>capbellpia</u> in all Member States.
> A (16) <u>vetcriide</u> shall be binding, as to the result to be achieved, upon each (17) <u>beermm</u> State to which it is addressed, but shall leave to the national authorities the choice of form and methods.
>
> *from Article 189, the Treaty of Rome*

8.3 Are the following statements true or false? Find reasons for your answers in A and B opposite.

1 Member states are required to incorporate European legislation into national law and to recognise the jurisdiction of the European Court of Justice in matters of EU law.
2 The national legislation of Member States takes precedence over Community rules.
3 The Common Customs Tariff applies to all goods imported by countries like Japan and the USA from the EU.
4 EU law prevents Member States from charging importers for bringing goods into that State from another Member State.

Over to you

How has membership of the EU affected a jurisdiction you are familiar with?

For access to European Union legislation, including Treaties and case law (for example, Costa v ENEL), go to EUR-Lex at: http://eur-lex.europa.eu/en/index.htm

9 Solicitors

A Legal practitioners

Lawyers in the United Kingdom jurisdictions generally **practise as solicitors** in private **firms**, **as legal advisers** in corporations, government departments, and advice agencies, or **as barristers** (see Unit 10). They can each **do advocacy**, **draft** legal **documents** and give written advice, but solicitors, unlike barristers, cannot **appear in** every **court**.

Traditionally, solicitors **undertake work** such as **conveyancing** (see Unit 40), and **drawing up contracts** (see Units 31–41) and **wills**. Barristers spend more time in court and **have a right of audience** in the higher courts. Unlike solicitors, barristers cannot usually be employed directly by clients but are **instructed** by solicitors. Solicitors normally **form partnerships** with other solicitors and work in offices with support staff. The qualification and **practice** of solicitors are regulated by the Law Society.

B Training

Sami, a 25 year-old **graduate**, is talking about his experience as a **trainee**.

'My first **degree** was in engineering at Manchester University. Then I did two one-year law courses. The first led to the Common Professional Examination, or CPE; the second was the Legal Practice Course. I had a vacation **placement** at Applewood Branston, who offered me a two-year **traineeship**. They have a six seat system, which is quite common. Trainees spend time attached to different law departments, which suits me as I get a basic grounding in the main departments of the firm, helping me find which area of the law I'd like to **specialise in**. I can work in four or more different areas of law for four months at a time and then decide on a **specialism** later in the **training contract**. In my third seat, in Corporate Finance, I've learnt a lot from being **on secondment** with a client and got excellent back up from my seat supervisor, that is, **supervising partner**. It was good to put the professional skills training into practice straight away.'

C A partner in a law firm

Hélène, from Monaco, is an *avocat* **admitted to** the Paris **Bar** – the professional association for lawyers. She **graduated** with a Bachelor of Law (LLB) in Paris and **obtained a Master's Degree** (LLM) in European Law from University College, London. She is a graduate of the Paris Institut d'Études Politiques.

'**I joined** Applewood Branston two years ago and was promoted to **partner** in the corporate and banking team in Paris. Before that I worked for twelve years for other leading international law firms. I've got extensive experience of **privatisations**, **mergers and acquisitions**, and I advise investment banks and **corporates**.'

9.1 A potential Polish client is talking to an English solicitor. Complete the solicitor's statements (1–3). Look at A opposite to help you. There is more than one possibility for one of the answers.

> I'm looking for a lawyer to help me buy some land for a business.

1 My firm undertakes a lot of .... We could advise you and help to .... contracts.

> We've had some trouble in the past with getting large invoices paid.

2 We can do .... If your case goes to court, we have .... and I can .... in the lower courts.

> Can you appear in the Appeal Court?

3 No, I'm a .... but my firm would instruct a .... if a case were to go to the Appeal Court.

9.2 Complete the table with words from A, B and C opposite and related forms. Put a stress mark in front of the stressed syllable in each word. The first one has been done for you.

Verb	Noun	Noun – person
'partner	'partnership	'partner
		trainee
advise		
	practice	
specialise		

9.3 Ana García is talking about her career. Complete what she says with words from the table above and B and C opposite. There is more than one possibility for one of the answers.

I'm an *abogada*, a lawyer in Spain. I obtained my law (1) .... in Barcelona. In the summers, as a student, I did a vacation (2) .... in my uncle's law (3) .... I (4) .... from university six years ago. Because my English and French are good I got a (5) .... to the New York office of my firm. While I was there I was (6) .... by the mergers and acquisitions team. I've always enjoyed working with large companies so now I want to (7) .... in (8) ....

Over to you

Write or talk to someone about your experience of legal education and training.
For information on the work of solicitors and links to other international professional organisations, go to: www.lawsociety.org.uk/home.law and the International Bar Association: www.ibanet.org/.

10 Barristers

A Organisation

Sylvia Garrison, a practising **barrister,** is describing the training and organisation of the profession.

'There are currently around 9,000 barristers **in practice** in England and Wales. Unlike solicitors, barristers can't form partnerships but must act as **sole traders** with **unlimited liability.** Some barristers are in employed practice and may only represent their employer, for example as **in-house counsel** or in government departments like the Crown Prosecution Service. Many work independently in **self-employed practice** in groups called **chambers** or **sets** and **practise at the Bar as a barrister.** Chambers are traditionally located in the four Inns of Court in London – Gray's Inn, Lincoln's Inn, Middle Temple, and Inner Temple – and are also located in the UK regions, known as **circuits.** The Inns are principally non-academic societies which provide collegiate and educational resources for barristers and **trainees.** Members of chambers, known as **tenants,** share common expenses and support services, which are administered by an administrative manager known as the **Clerk,** along with ancillary staff such as secretaries.

A barrister's main work is to **provide representation** in the courts, where they are referred to as counsel, to **draft documents** associated with court procedure, and to **give opinions,** that is, specialist legal advice. They are normally **instructed** by solicitors or other recognised professionals, such as patent agents or Legal Advice Centres, on behalf of **lay clients.** As the law has become more complex, barristers increasingly specialise in particular areas, such as personal injury, crime, family or commercial law. A number of Specialist Bar Associations, also known as SBAs, support and represent members. Barristers are governed by the General Council of the Bar, known as the **Bar Council,** and the **Inns of Court.**'

> BrE: chamber/set; ScotE: stable
> BrE: barrister; ScotE: advocate; AmE: trial lawyer / appellate attorney

B Training and qualifications of practising barristers

'Intending barristers need a qualifying law degree, for example a **Bachelor of Laws,** also known as an **LLB.** However, many students graduate in a non-law subject and undertake a one year **conversion course** known as a **postgraduate Diploma in Law,** or **GDL.** The student barrister then applies to join one of the Inns of Court to study for the **Bar Vocational Course,** or **BVC.** It's also mandatory for students to **keep terms,** which means dining at their Inn a fixed number of times, before they can be **called to the Bar,** that is, qualify as a barrister. Then the new barrister faces intense competition to obtain a funded **pupillage** in chambers for twelve months in order to get practical training. All applicants are advised first to **do a mini-pupillage** of one or two weeks to get some insight into what being a pupil is like. Pupillage, known as devilling in Scotland, is divided into two parts – a **non-practising** six months when pupils **shadow their pupil master,** an experienced barrister, by observing professional activities, and the second, practising six months when pupils, with their supervisor's permission, can undertake to **supply legal services** and **exercise rights of audience,** in other words, speak in court. To gain a Full Qualification Certificate pupils must learn the rules of conduct and etiquette at the Bar, learn to prepare and present a case competently, learn to **draft pleadings** and **opinions,** have **advocacy training,** and pass a **forensic accountancy** course which covers the use of financial information in litigation. If successful at the end of the twelve months, the qualified barrister applies for a **tenancy** in chambers. When a **junior barrister** has practised at the Bar for 10 to 15 years, it's possible to apply to become a **senior barrister,** or Queen's Counsel (QC), whose work concentrates on court appearances, advocacy, and opinions.'

10.1 Match the two parts of the definitions. Look at A opposite to help you.

1 Someone who works for his or herself is
2 If you speak on behalf of clients in court, you
3 Non-professional clients are known as
4 Barristers working solely for a company are called
5 The governing authorities of barristers are
6 When a solicitor gives a barrister the details of a case, the barrister is
7 When you work as a barrister you

a provide representation.
b lay clients.
c self-employed / a sole trader.
d instructed.
e in-house counsel.
f practise at the Bar.
g the Bar Council and the Inns of Court.

10.2 Complete the extracts from a trainee barrister describing her professional life. Look at A and B opposite to help you. There is more than one possibility for two of the answers.

I took a first degree in Modern History, then did the (1) .... in law at City University, which was much harder. I then did the (2) .... at the Inns of Court School of Law.

Most days I'd expect to be present in (3) .... from about 8.45 am to 7.00 pm, working almost throughout in my (4) ....'s room. During that time I (5) .... his professional life completely.

I generally look at papers when they first come in. I'm expected to be able to suggest how the case might be approached. In a week I might draft a (6) .... , prepare notes for a conference with clients, comment on draft witness statements, and research legal points.

Although all (7) .... are for twelve months, if they think you have no prospect of finding a (8) .... in the chambers, after six months you would be told discreetly.

Chambers runs (9) .... training evenings to reduce the loss of opportunity to (10) .... in court.

When I've practised for more than ten years, I'd be interested in being appointed as a (11) .... , with a specialist area such as employment law.

Over to you

Explain the organisation of your profession as if you were speaking to a fellow legal practitioner.

For more information on barristers, go to the Bar Council: www.barcouncil.org.uk/.

11 Working lives

A A company commercial lawyer

Sophie Brettle is talking about her work at Melton Deans.

'I'm a **partner** in a medium-sized regional law firm, working within the Company Commercial Department. I **head up** a team of eight, comprising six lawyers and two **paralegals** – legal researchers – undertaking projects work for **Public Sector** clients. Our main client is a Government Department. We're **instructed** by them to advise and act on Private Finance Initiative Projects, also known as the PFI. This involves negotiating with a number of other parties comprising the funders, the building contractors, and facilities management and ensuring that the client's aims and objectives are met and their **best interests protected**.

A **significant proportion of** my time is spent in **all parties meetings**. As these transactions are complex, and the meetings are attended by all sides and their legal advisers, I have to make sure **comprehensive notes** are taken by an assistant solicitor. Following a meeting, documents reflecting the **terms agreed** are prepared and circulated for approval.

An all parties meeting

Within the practice, I'm a member of the Executive Committee and have responsibility for aspects of financial management within the department. I also deal with recruitment, training, and development within the department. During a working day as a **fee earner**, I have to combine my **chargeable work** for clients with administrative duties.'

B A legal secretary

An assistant solicitor is instructing Marie Lapotaire, the Commercial Department's **legal secretary**:

Solicitor: I've just sent you some **sound files with the minutes on** from yesterday's meeting. Is there any way you can **type** those **up** before anything else? I know you've got **a substantial amount of** work at the moment.

Marie: No problem. Do you want me to **circulate them by email** as soon as I've finished, **get a hard copy** and put it on the file?

Solicitor: Please. I'm going to be running between meetings for **a large part of** the day but if I get a minute, I'll have a quick look at the hard copy and **mark** it **up** with any changes. Don't wait for me to do that before **getting the draft out** – there are **action points** that the paralegals need to be **getting on with**.

Marie: Fine, I'll **copy everyone in**. Anything else? I've put all the documentation for Project Angel on your desk. I don't know if it's **ready to go out** yet?

Solicitor: I saw that, thanks. No, I need to make sure that the client is happy with the latest clauses the funder wants. Also, I think they may have negotiated more concessions so I'll have to **get back to you** on those.

Marie: OK. By the way, I think your **out of office message** is still on, although the date's wrong. Don't worry, I'll change it. Your calls are still coming through to my phone so I'll carry on **taking messages**.

11.1 Make word combinations from A opposite using words from the box. Then use appropriate word combinations to complete Sophie Brettle's sentences below.

fee	terms	interests	work	comprehensive	best
chargeable	notes	meeting	earner	agreed	all parties

1
> I don't think we can accept that clause. It's not in the ....
> .... of the client.

2
> Marie, can you go ahead and set up the next ....
> .... ?
> We need everyone to be there.

3
> Will you check the ....
> .... match the notes taken from the meeting with the contractors and client?

4
> We can't spend any more time on this. It's not ....
> ....

11.2 Find three expressions in A and B opposite which can be used in the combinations below to mean 'a lot of'.

....

.... my time / my week / my workload

....

11.3 Marie Lapotaire is talking about her working day. Replace the underlined words and phrases with alternative words and phrases from B opposite. Pay attention to the grammatical context. There is more than one possibility for one of the answers.

> In addition to typing up (1) recorded notes from meetings, (2) sending a copy to everyone by email, and (3) printing off emails, most days I'll be given various other tasks to carry out, such as document generation. If the solicitor (4) indicates changes on a draft text, I'll (5) word process them. I sometimes have to get addresses and contact details from the Internet and make appointments for meetings or conference calls. Obviously, I also take incoming calls when the fee earners aren't available and I let the caller know the solicitor will (6) call them back. I'll also (7) continue with any other tasks she's given me. Once a month I attend the secretarial committee as the representative for my department.

Over to you

What is your function within your organisation? Talk about your responsibilities and a typical working day or week.

For information on the work of solicitors in specific law firms in the UK, go to: www.venables.co.uk/.

12 Judges

Judicial appointments in England and Wales

Judicial Office	Court (see Unit 4)	Number
Lords of Appeal in Ordinary (also known as **Law Lords**)	House of Lords	12
Lord Justices of Appeal	Court of Appeal	37
High Court Judges	High Court of Justice	107
Circuit Judges	Crown Court and County Court	638
Recorders	Crown Court and County Court	1359
District Judges (Civil)	County Court	422
Deputy District Judges (Civil)	County Court	751
District Judges (also known as Stipendiary Magistrates)	Magistrates' Court	139
Deputy District Judges	Magistrates' Court	148

Note: **Recorders** generally hear less complex or serious cases than Circuit Judges and start by sitting in the Crown Court. After two years they might sit in the County Court.
Number of judges listed in above table correct as of 27/11/06. See www.judiciary.gov.uk/.

An Act of Parliament **lays down** the **mandatory requirements** for most **judicial offices**. Candidates must have practised as a lawyer or judge for a specified time and must meet other statutory requirements for specific posts. The **hierarchical** structure of the courts informs the process of selection to **the Judiciary**. Experience gained as a judge in a lower court is one of the qualifications for appointment to a higher court. Senior appointments to the Court of Appeal and the High Court are made by the Queen following the recommendation of the Prime Minister, currently on the advice of the **Lord Chancellor** – a senior member of the government and head of the judicial system.

B The training of judges

The Judicial Studies Board (JSB) is responsible for the training of judges, lay magistrates, and members of Tribunals in England and Wales. The JSB would normally organise the following for an appointee Recorder in the Crown Court: an **induction course;** visits to **penal establishments**, for example prison and young offender institutions; meetings with personnel from the **Probation Service**, which deals with criminals, often young offenders, who are not sent to prison unless they reoffend, but who are under the supervision of a **probation officer**.

The appointee would experience a period of sitting in on **the Bench** – the judge's area of the Court – with a Circuit Judge. In his first week after appointment he would be supervised by a Circuit Judge. Practical guidelines for judges are set out in **Bench Books**.

C Civil courts: sentencing and court orders

Judges in **civil courts** can **fine, commit to imprisonment** (normally between 28 days and six months) or give a **suspended sentence** – where imprisonment does not take place unless the offender commits another offence. An **applicant** can **seek an injunction** – an order – against a **respondent**. The court may grant an **interim injunction**, that is, a temporary one, to stop the defendant from doing something before the **hearing of the application**. The judge can **grant** or **refuse an injunction** against a legal person to do or not do specified acts. The judge can, alternatively, require **an undertaking**, or promise, from the relevant **party** at the hearing proceedings.

12.1 Match the judicial offices in the box with the required qualifications below (1–4). Bear in mind the hierachical structure of the courts. Look at A opposite to help you.

Lord of Appeal in Ordinary	Lord Justice of Appeal
Circuit Judge	District Judge (Magistrates' Court)

1 must have been qualified as a lawyer for at least seven years
2 must have been qualified for ten years, although three years' service as a full-time District Judge is allowed
3 must have been qualified as a lawyer for at least 15 years and is usually drawn from judges in the Courts of Appeal in England, Wales, and Northern Ireland, and in the Court of Session in Scotland
4 the statutory qualification is at least ten years in the High Court as a lawyer and, in practice, to be a High Court Judge

12.2 Complete the definitions. Look at A and B opposite to help you.

1 .... – collective word for a group of judges and the name of the place where a judge sits in court
2 .... – formal collective word for all the judges in the legal system
3 .... – the specific post of a judge (for example, a High Court Judge)
4 .... – place where people are held as a punishment when convicted of an offence.

12.3 Complete the sentences. Look at C opposite to help you.

1 Judges may make a first sentence for a non-serious offence a .... sentence.
2 The period of .... awarded by the judge should reflect the number and seriousness of the offences and their context.
3 A person who seeks an injunction is generally described as the ....

4 Instead of ordering a specific act, the court can seek the agreement of the relevant party to an .... to do the specified act.
5 An applicant may seek an .... to prevent a breach of contract.
6 If an applicant claims that the defendant is about to do something that infringes his/her rights before there can be a hearing (for example, to dispose of disputed property), the judge may grant an ....

Over to you

Describe the appointment and training of judges in your legal system. What powers of sentencing do judges have?

For more information on judges in the UK, go to: www.jsboard.co.uk/, www.dca.gov.uk/judicial/ and www.judiciary.gov.uk/.

A law firm's structure and practice

A | A law firm's structure and practice

Anchor Robbins, a large UK law firm, is **submitting a tender for the provision of legal services to** a local authority. In the first section of the tender document, the firm's structure and breadth of **expertise** is set out. Typically, descriptions of law firms' practice areas and expertise are in strongly positive language.

---

1 ANCHOR ROBBINS' RESOURCES AND EXPERTISE

1.1 General Details

Personnel
282 personnel **including** 38 partners, 62 solicitors, 12 other lawyers, 14 legal executives, and 10 trainee solicitors, in addition to clerical, secretarial, and support staff.

Structure
We have three specialist areas:
Commercial Property incorporates Public Sector, Construction, Planning and Environment.
Company Commercial comprises Banking, Project Finance, Procurement, Employment and Pensions.
Private Client offers Wills, Trusts and Probate, Tax Planning, and Residential Conveyancing.

Dedicated specialist dispute resolution services are provided within each of the respective areas.

Services
We provide all the services you require. The head of our Projects team, Jan Stephenson, will **lead** the team providing legal services to you.

1.2 Professional Indemnity Insurance

We have provided full details of our current **professional indemnity cover** in our **Pre-Qualification Questionnaire (PPQ)**. The terms of our cover are **reviewed annually**.

1.3 Resources and Specialist Knowledge

Expertise and Structure:
Each of our **departments contains specialist partner-led teams** ensuring that we are able to **resource high quality specialist knowledge** and **provide a comprehensive service to** our clients. Further details of our Projects Team are set out at (3) below.

Commitment:
We are committed to anticipating our clients' needs and meeting them. **Fundamental to** this is the commitment of each team leader to understand thoroughly the priorities and business of our clients.

Information Technology:
We have **made significant investment in** our information technology systems in order to give the support and resources that our lawyers need. Our systems enable us to **transfer know-how into** a searchable database using links to cases and legislation, to **monitor workloads**, **measure outputs**, and plan ahead more effectively. The stability and security of our system is of particular importance to our clients and to us.

Projects at Anchor Robbins:
The Projects team is **headed up** by Jan Stephenson and brings together specialists in infrastructure, construction, energy, planning, and public sector. The team are able to **draw on relevant expertise from** elsewhere in the firm when required and **have exclusive access to** a dedicated Professional Support Lawyer.

The team have **had extensive experience in** handling PFI (Private Finance Initiative) since its very beginning and have been **involved in** a considerable range of accommodation projects including schools, hospitals, courts, and light rail projects.

Note: **legal executives** are qualified to assist solicitors but do not practise as solicitors.
procurement – procedures, which may include use of a **PPQ**, by which public authorities award contracts for the provision of public works, supplies, and services in accordance with rules and regulations.
Private Finance Initiative (PFI) – collaboration between government and private sector companies to fund and develop major public infrastructure such as roads, schools, and hospitals.

13.1 Complete the sentences with verbs from A opposite. Pay attention to the grammatical context. There is more than one possibility for all of the answers.

1 The company .... a wide range of services to international corporate clients.
2 Rattigan's employment practice .... six partners, 14 associates and 11 other legal and support staff.
3 Our outstanding commercial litigation practice area .... insurance and reinsurance litigation, securities and commodities disputes, partnership law, bankruptcy, and business torts.
4 Our finance department .... lawyers who excel in cross-border transactions.
5 Our experienced mergers and acquisitions team is .... Miguel Ortiz, who graduated in law at the University Complutense in Madrid and gained his LLM from ESADE.

13.2 Find verbs in A opposite that can be used to make word combinations with the phrases in the box. More than one verb may sometimes be possible. Then use appropriate word combinations to complete the sentences below. Pay attention to the grammatical context.

relevant expertise	exclusive access	extensive experience
a comprehensive service	significant investment	specialist knowledge

1 The litigation team .... in handling complex international disputes.
2 Our firm has .... in knowledge management systems, enabling staff to access an extensive database.
3 Clients are able to .... from dedicated teams in each practice area.
4 Due to the expertise of our staff we can .... in commercial litigation in a number of jurisdictions.
5 We can .... to domestic and multinational clients, with particular expertise in corporate and finance.

13.3 Complete the definitions. Look at A opposite to help you.

1 .... – staff
2 .... – put in a formal proposal to win a contract with an estimate of the cost
3 .... – insurance to protect your business against compensation sought by a client for harm or damage caused by mistake or negligence by an employee of your firm
4 ....-............................... – move specialist knowledge
5 .... – evaluate work done

Over to you

Describe the structure and practice of a law firm you are familiar with or would like to work for.

For information on legal executives, go to: www.ilex.org.uk/; for information on European Public Procurement Directives, go to: www.eel.nl/ and carry out a search.

14 Client care procedures

Explaining client care procedures

Greg Spenser is a South African lawyer taking part in an exchange programme with Bridgeman Banks, a **sister firm** in London. During his first week, John Coleman, the partner supervising him, is explaining the firm's **client care procedures**.

'One of the first things you'll need to do on any new matter is a **client care letter**. As most of the **clients** you will be **acting for** will be existing corporate clients, you won't need to **carry out any identification procedures**, although you should be aware of them. They're all **set out in** the **office manual**, in the risk management section.

A client care letter should **refer to the matter on which you are instructed to act** and should set out the basic aims and the **agreed target timescale**, such as there is. In the letter you must inform the client of who will be **undertaking work** for them and give the name of the person with **overall responsibility for** conduct of the matter. In fact, the **letters** are normally **prepared as if** they're from that person. We also inform clients that we have a partner who they can contact **in the event that they have a complaint** which they feel cannot be dealt with by the person supervising the file, although obviously we hope that that **eventuality** will not **arise**.

The letter should **provide a fee estimate** for work by staff and should also **give the details of any anticipated disbursements**, such as court fees, search fees, and other costs. If it isn't possible to give a quote **at the outset**, or start, **of** a matter you may, for example, suggest that you **obtain their approval** before undertaking any work **in excess of an agreed limit**. You must agree to provide an estimate **at the earliest opportunity** and **in the meantime** let the client know what **costs** are being **incurred**.

There are **precedent letters** in the **department manual** that you can access via the Intranet. I would refer to those rather than the **hard copies**, as they're **updated** regularly on the system. Your secretary should be familiar with the letters so you need only give her the information specific to this matter in order for her to **prepare the first draft**.

As a firm we're Lexcel **compliant**. Basically this means we **conform to a standard** approved by Lexcel and have incorporated their requirements into our systems, including those for file management. **As well as giving quality assurance to** our clients, our **accreditation** does make a difference to our **indemnity insurance premium. As far as the insurers are concerned**, the risk of a claim is lessened by the fact that we can demonstrate to an **external auditor** that we **have** effective **risk management procedures in place**.'

Note: identification procedures – regulations controlling identity checks on clients (see Unit 15)
Lexcel compliant – indicates that a firm has the practice management quality mark of the Law Society (England and Wales). To find out about Lexcel, go to:
www.lawsociety.org.uk/professional/practicesupport/lexcel.law

14.1 Complete the definitions. Look at A opposite to help you. There is more than one possibility for one of the answers.

1 .... – a handbook of instructions in your place of work
2 .... – models of standard correspondence
3 .... – costs to be charged to the client
4 .... – fee for protection against compensation awards
   for damages
5 .... – outside assessor who checks procedures comply with standards
   and regulations

14.2 Match the highlighted clauses in this extract from a client care precedent letter (a–f) with the instructions for writing a client care precedent letter given by the supervising partner in A opposite. The first one has been done for you.

> Dear [   ]
>
> [Ref:]
>
> [a]I refer to [   ] when you confirmed our instructions to act for you in this matter. I will be pleased to do so on your behalf.
>
> 1 **INSTRUCTIONS**
>   1.1 Your instructions are [to ....   ].
>   1.2 This will involve :-
>   *[list issues, advice, action to be taken as set out in the file note on client]*
>
> 2 **TIMESCALE**
>   2.1 [b]The likely timescale of this transaction is [   ].
>
> 3 **PERSONNEL**
>   3.1 [c]I will deal with this matter personally and I am a solicitor with the firm.
>   [d]John Coleman will be the partner with overall responsibility for supervision of the matter.
>   If for any reason I am unavailable please ask for my secretary, Aida Muñoz.
>
> 4 **COSTS**
>   4.1 [e]In a matter such as this it is difficult to estimate the probable total charges as this depends on a range of factors beyond our control such as the conduct of the other side. We have therefore agreed that I will monitor our charges and when costs reach £[.........] plus VAT and disbursements no further work will be done without your prior consent.
>   [f]As soon as it becomes practicable to do so, I will provide you with an estimate as to the likely total charges and expenses.

In a client care letter you should...
(a) – ... refer to the matter on which you are instructed to act ...

14.3 There are many ways of using 'as' in English and it occurs frequently in legal texts. It can function as a preposition, as a conjunction, and it can introduce a subordinate clause. Match the underlined examples from A opposite (1–5) with the appropriate synonym for its use in the text (a–f).

1 <u>As</u> most of the clients you will be acting for will be ...
2 ... letters are normally prepared <u>as if</u> they're from ...
3 <u>As</u> a firm we're Lexcel compliant ...
4 <u>As well as</u> giving quality assurance to our clients ...
5 ... <u>as far as</u> the insurers <u>are concerned</u>, the risk ...

a in addition to
b from the perspective of
c because
d on the basis that
e in the context of being

Over to you

Talk or write about the client care procedures you are familiar with as if to a colleague working for another firm. Describe your experience of professional quality assurance schemes.

15 Money laundering procedures

A Money laundering procedures

Below are extracts from a statutory instrument that has implications for law firms.

Statutory Instruments 2003 No.3075

The Money Laundering Regulations 2003

PART II
OBLIGATIONS ON PERSONS WHO CARRY ON RELEVANT BUSINESS

Systems and training etc. to prevent money laundering

3. – (1) Every person must in the course of relevant business carried on by him in the United Kingdom –

(a) **comply with** the requirements of regulations 4 (**identification procedures**), 6 (**record keeping procedures**) and 7 (**internal reporting procedures**);

(b) establish such other procedures of internal control and communication as may be appropriate for the purposes of **forestalling** and preventing money laundering; and

(c) **take appropriate measures** so that relevant employees are –

(i) **made aware of** the provisions of these Regulations, Part 7 of the **Proceeds of** Crime Act 2002 (**money laundering**) and sections 18 and 21A of the Terrorism Act 2000[24]; and

(ii) given training in how to recognise and **deal with transactions** which may be related to money laundering.

(2) A person who **contravenes this regulation** is guilty of an offence and liable –

(a) on conviction on indictment, to imprisonment for a term not exceeding 2 years, to a **fine** or to both;

(b) on summary conviction, to a fine not exceeding the statutory minimum.

---

(5) In proceedings against any person for an **offence under this regulation**, it is a defence for that person to show that he **took all reasonable steps** and **exercised all due diligence** to avoid committing the offence.

Identification procedures

4. – (1) In this regulation and in regulations 5 to 7 –

(a) "A" means a person who carries on relevant business in the United Kingdom; and

(b) "B" means an applicant for business.

(2) This regulation applies if –

(a) A and B **form**, or agree to form, **a business relationship**;

(b) in respect of any **one-off transaction** –

(i) A knows or **suspects** that the transaction **involves money laundering**; or

(ii) payment of 15,000 euro or more is to be made by or to B; or

(c) in respect of two or more one-off transactions, it appears to A (whether at the outset or subsequently) that the transactions are linked and involve, in total, the payment of 15,000 euro or more by or to B.

(3) A must **maintain identification procedures** which –

(a) require that **as soon as is reasonably practicable** after contact is first made between A and B –

(i) B must **produce satisfactory evidence** of his **identity**; or

(ii) such measures **specified in** the procedures must be taken in order to produce satisfactory evidence of B's identity;

(b) **take into account** the greater potential for money laundering which arises when B is not physically present when being **identified**;

(c) require that where satisfactory evidence of identity is not obtained, the business relationship or one-off transaction must not proceed any further; and

(d) require that where B acts or appears to **act for another person**, reasonable measures must be taken for the purpose of establishing the identity of that person.

Regulation 7

Internal reporting procedures

(1) A must **maintain internal reporting procedures** which require that –

(a) a person in A's organisation is **nominated to receive disclosures** under this regulation ("the nominated officer").

Note: Headings in the above document appear in bold in the original statutory instrument.

15.1 Complete the definitions. Look at A opposite to help you.

1 .... – process by which finance obtained through crime is used in such a way that it appears to originate from a legitimate source
2 ....-........................ .... – a business activity not carried out in the course of an existing business relationship
3 .... – anticipating and hindering
4 .... – as quickly as possible
5 .... – took every care and carried out required procedures
6 .... – confidential information made public

15.2 Replace the underlined words and phrases in the memo below with alternative words and phrases from A opposite. Pay attention to the grammatical context.

BRIDGEMAN BANKS – INTERNAL MEMORANDUM

To: All Partners and Fee Earners   **Date: 23 April 2007**
From: Peter O'Donnell
Subject: Money laundering procedures

You will no doubt be aware of the serious implications for legal firms and their employees of failing to (1) <u>observe</u> the (2) <u>Profits from</u> Crime Act and the Money Laundering Regulations. Given that it is possible to become unintentionally involved in a money laundering transaction in the course of, for example, a property purchase, or in a situation where you (3) <u>carry out activities on behalf of someone else</u>, the firm is anxious to put in place systems and to provide training to ensure that there are effective procedures so that employees do not risk (4) <u>breaking</u> the regulation. The penalties following criminal prosecution and conviction may comprise imprisonment and a (5) <u>money penalty</u>. We need to be able to demonstrate that we (6) <u>did what was possible</u> and (7) <u>carried out all formal requirements</u> to avoid committing an offence. The main offences under the current legislation are:

▸ Not (8) <u>hindering</u> or preventing a money laundering arrangement
▸ Not making a (9) <u>statement</u> if you know or (10) <u>guess</u> money laundering
▸ Prejudicing an investigation, for example by tipping off a suspect

Evidence of identity
As you know, the precedent form of the Client Care letter for new clients and the firm's standard terms of business contain information to make clients (11) <u>conscious</u> of our obligations under the legislation. An important part of our procedures is the requirement to produce (12) <u>sufficient proof</u> of identity from new clients as soon as is reasonably practicable. Obviously there are different requirements (for example, appearance in person, passport, driving licence, etc.) for different types of client and the relevant guidance is set out in the Office Manual.

What to do if you are suspicious – internal reporting procedures
I am the firm's (13) <u>named</u> Money Laundering Reporting Officer. If you have any suspicions at all, either about a particular client or any aspect of a (14) <u>business activity</u>, please feel free to contact me. If I think we need to refer the matter to the National Criminal Intelligence Service, it is extremely unlikely we will be able to inform the client – this can amount to tipping off. If NCIS decides to investigate, we will have to terminate our retainer with the client.

Over to you

Explain how money laundering is dealt with in a jurisdiction you are familiar with, as if to a foreign colleague.

To see the Money Laundering Regulations 2003 and Proceeds of Crime Act 2002, go to:
www.opsi.gov.uk/acts.htm

16 Client correspondence

Client correspondence

Conciseness can be a feature of legal correspondence in English. This is partly achieved by using words or phrases to refer to segments of earlier text (substitution) or by not completing a phrase and omitting words (ellipsis), assuming the reader can recover the meaning from the preceding text. Another feature of legal text is the use of capitals mid-sentence for key terms which may be defined or interpreted elsewhere in the text or in another document. The letter below is from a sequence of correspondence between a solicitor and his client. It concerns the final stages of the purchase of a company.

JENKINS WATSON
Strictly Private and Confidential

Mr G Stobbard
Managing Director
Lincoln James Limited
4 India Street
Winchester

aep/2122-004
Encl/.

23 February 2007

Dear Gordon

Project Ivory
Target Company – Franklin Red Limited (FR Ltd)

Following our meeting on Monday **please find enclosed** the further **amended** *Heads of Terms* relating to **the above** for your approval.

As previously discussed, you will let me have further instructions **in relation to** conditions to which *Completion* will be subject. You will see that I have left **this aspect** as originally drafted **for the time being**.

I should be grateful if you would read **the enclosed** carefully and confirm that you are happy with **the same**, or alternatively let me know if any **further** changes are required. I will be engaged in meetings on Thursday morning but am in the office **for the rest of the week apart from that**.

I look forward to hearing from you.

Yours sincerely

Alex Paine

Alex Paine

Note: Encl/. – an abbreviation for 'Enclosure', used to indicate that other documents are included
Heads of Terms – document setting out the principal agreement pre-contract
completion – financial closure of the deal; when it is completed

Standard phrases for starting and ending letters and emails

Stating the reason for writing
I am writing to inform/advise you that …
Please find enclosed … / I am pleased to enclose …
We act for / on behalf of …
We are instructed by the above-named client
in relation to …

Referring to previous contact
Further to our recent correspondence …
I write further to my letter / our meeting of …
As previously discussed …
Following our meeting on …
Thank you for your letter/email of …

Offering further assistance
Please let me know if you have any particular concerns …
Please let me know if we can be of further assistance …
If you have any questions, please do not hesitate to give me a call …

Referring to the next step
I should/would be grateful if you could …
Could you please confirm that …

Ending
I look forward to hearing from you shortly / as soon as possible.
I look forward to our meeting / your reply.

16.1 Match the words and phrases from the letter in A opposite (1–6) with the synonyms (a–f).

1 apart from	a for now
2 for the rest of	b changed
3 enclosed	c besides
4 further	d for the remainder of
5 for the time being	e additional
6 amended	f together with the letter

16.2 Decide which of the following phrases underlined in A opposite is an example of substitution and which is an example of ellipsis. In the case of substitution, make a note of the phrase in the letter which it refers back to. In the case of ellipsis, make a note of the missing word(s). The first one has been done for you.

1 … for the rest of the week apart from <u>that</u>.
  Substitution of 'that' for 'Thursday morning'
2 … relating to <u>the above</u> …
3 … I have left <u>this aspect</u> as originally drafted …
4 … read <u>the enclosed</u> carefully …
5 … and confirm that you are happy with <u>the same</u>, or …

16.3 Read A opposite then say if these statements are true or false. Find reasons for your answers in the letter.

1 The Heads of Terms have been changed several times.
2 Alex Paine has made no changes to the conditions for Completion.
3 Alex Paine is not expecting his client to give him more instructions.
4 Alex Paine does not expect his client to reply if he is satisfied with the enclosed document.

16.4 Complete this letter from Alex Paine to his client with appropriate phrases from B opposite. There is more than one possibility for three of the answers.

> 6 April 2007
>
> Dear Gordon
>
> **Project Ivory**
> **Target Company – Franklin Red Limited (FR Ltd)**
>
> (1) .... (*state the reason for writing*) the Agreement in respect of the above which has now been agreed by FR Ltd's solicitors. This has not changed since the last version sent to you by email. As (2) .... (*refer to previous contact*) please note in particular details concerning employees in Schedule 5. I don't think there are any surprises there but (3) .... (*offer further assistance*).
>
> If you are happy with the same, (4) .... (*refer to the next step*) arrange for the Agreement to be executed on behalf of Lincoln James Ltd where indicated. Please bring the executed Agreement along to our meeting on Monday 11th.
> (5) .... (*ending phrase*).
>
> Kind regards,
>
> *Alex Paine*
>
> Alex Paine

Over to you

Look for examples of substitution and ellipsis in correspondence and practise decoding them. Make a note of standard phrases you notice in correspondence from English-speaking colleagues or clients.

17 Explanations and clarification

A Explaining a procedure

When you list the different stages of a procedure, your listeners' comprehension of the information that you are presenting will be better if you use phrases to structure and signpost what you say. For example:

First …, then …, next …, after that …, finally …

Other phrases you might use include:

The next thing/step is to …, once that's been done …, before that happens you/we …, the last step will be to …

B Approximating and comparing

When talking to or writing to a client or colleague from another legal system, you may need to explain or describe features of your system which are different or broadly similar. The phrases below can be used to compare aspects of your system. It may be appropriate to use key terms in your own language and then offer a comparative explanation, for example:

> In Scotland 'delict' arises from the law of obligations. **This is comparable to** 'tort' in England.

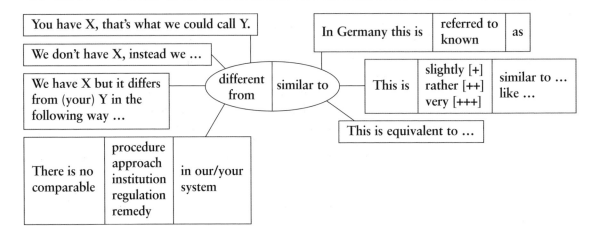

C Rephrasing and clarifying

When you are explaining something which is new or complex, it is important to check that your listeners understand what may be new terms or concepts. You can help their comprehension by rephrasing your words and help your own comprehension of what they say by rephrasing or summarising their words. You can use the phrases below to signal that you are rephrasing or asking for clarification.

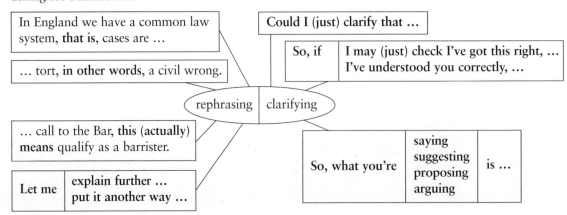

17.1 Explain the different stages in getting proprietary rights for an invention as if to a client. Look at A opposite and use the information below to help you. The first part of the explanation has been done for you.

- consider submitting an application to the patent office in the research phase
- don't publicly disclose the invention because this might be interpreted as prior publication
- think about using the services of a registered patent agent to help prepare the specification (the legal document) required by the patent office
- complete the form 'Request for grant of patent'
- take or send the documents to the patent office
- the patent office decides whether the invention fulfils specific conditions before it grants a patent

You wanted me to give you an outline of the stages in getting proprietary rights. First, consider

submitting an application to the patent office in the research phase.

....

....

....

....

....

17.2 Complete the sentences with words and phrases from B opposite. Use the index to look up any unfamiliar terms. There is more than one possibility for four of the answers.

1 A bona fide act is .... an act in good faith.
2 The jury system in Scotland .... that in England because there are 15 jurors on a panel in Scotland compared with 12 in England.
3 In the English legal profession, those with rights of audience in all the courts are barristers; in Scotland they are .... advocates.
4 ALADI (Latin American Integration Association) is .... APEC (Asia Pacific Economic Cooperation) because it shares the aim of strengthening the trading system between its members.
5 In Scotland, juries may reach one of three verdicts: guilty, not guilty or not proven. This .... England where only two verdicts are possible: guilty or not guilty.

17.3 Complete the sentences with words and phrases from C opposite. There is more than one possibility for two of the answers.

1 The clause excludes abnormal weather conditions, ... , weather which is significantly different from previous records, like a hurricane.
2 Towards the end of the agreement there are usually the boiler-plate clauses, ... , clauses such as what the applicable law will be and the way in which notices have to be served.
3 During negotiations, arguments can often arise in connection with when a party has to perform an obligation. .... , disputes can happen over the interpretation of terms like: 'immediately', 'forthwith' and 'as soon as possible'.
4 You referred to the term 'forthwith'. .... you're saying the term is ambiguous?

Over to you

Use appropriate phrases from A to talk about a complicated legal procedure you have to manage in the course of your work. Or, compare an aspect of your country's legal system or law with an equivalent in the UK or the USA or another legal system.

18 Legalese

A   Legal language

Legal writing in English has developed over hundreds of years and is characterised by specific features, some of which can make it difficult for the non-lawyer to understand. Characteristics of legal writing include: using Latin terms (see text B below); using technical terms ('subsidiarity' – see Unit 8); using old-fashioned words not much in general use (see text C below); using pairs of words with a reciprocal relationship ('lessor'/'lessee' – see Unit 39); using legal jargon ('without prejudice to') including the use of pairs of words ('terms and conditions'), or triplets ('build, erect or construct'); having special meanings for words in ordinary use ('the judge determined the facts of the case', where 'determined' means 'decided'); using vague words ('provide a sufficient service'); using long sentences with little punctuation; inverting word order ('title absolute'); using capital letters to signal important or defined terms ('the terms of the Lease …') avoiding personal pronouns ('you', 'we', 'I'); the specific use of the modal verb **'shall'** to impose an obligation or duty on someone ('The tenant shall not sub-let the whole or part of the premises.'); the use of 'shall' in a directory sense ('Notice of an appeal shall be filed within 28 days.').

There is a movement to draft legal text in standard, modern, 'plain' English but any change will be slow.

Note: Some legal drafters argue that the use of 'shall' in a directory sense is to be avoided because of confusion. Note also the general English use of 'shall' to refer to future intentions ('I shall write to him'), although this use is increasingly uncommon.

B   Latin terms

There are many Latin terms in written English legal text, although recent reforms in the English justice system have encouraged the use of English rather than Latin. Some Latin terms are used so frequently that they are in general English use (**e.g., ad hoc, bona fide, pro rata, etc.**). It is useful to be able to recognise their meaning and a dictionary or online glossary will help. Forms of pronunciation vary.

ad hoc – for this purpose
affidavit – witnessed, signed statement
bona fide – in good faith
caveat – warning
de facto – in fact
de jure – by right
et cetera (etc.) – and so on
exempli gratia (e.g.) – for example
ex parte (ex p.) – by a party without notice
id est (i.e.) – that is
in camera – hearing a case in private
in curia – in open court

in situ – in its original situation
inter alia – among other things
ipso facto – by the fact
per pro – on behalf of another
per se – by itself
prima facie – at first sight
pro rata – in proportion
quasi – as if it were
sub judice – in the course of trial
ultra vires – beyond the power
videlicet (viz) – namely

C   Older words and modern equivalents

A number of linking terms are used in older written legal texts (case reports, legislation, court documentation, contracts, etc.) to refer to other parts of the same text, to different legal documents, or to related contexts.

the aforementioned / the foregoing – set out above / written above
the undermentioned – set out below / written below
hereafter – after this
hereby – in this way / by this
herein – in this (document)
hereof – of this
hereto – to this
herewith – with this

notwithstanding – despite
thereafter – after that
thereby – in that way / by that
therein – in that (document)
thereof – of that
thereto – to that
therewith – with that

18.1 Underline the characteristic features of legal writing mentioned in A opposite (for example, using old words) in the following consumer contract terms (1–3). Then complete the revised versions in plain terms (a–c) with appropriate words (or forms of words) from the original terms (1–3). Pay attention to the grammatical context.

1
This Agreement and the benefits and advantages herein contained are personal to each Member and shall not be sold, assigned or transferred by the Member.

a
.... is not transferable.

2
Lessor shall not be liable for loss of or damage to any property left, stored, or transported by Hirer or any other person in or upon Vehicle either before or after the return thereof to Lessor. Hirer hereby agrees to hold Lessor harmless from, and indemnify Lessor against all claims based on or arising out of such loss or damage unless caused by the negligence of Lessor.

b
We are only .... for .... or damage to .... left in the .... if the loss or damage .... from our ....

3
Title to property in the goods shall remain vested in the Company (notwithstanding the delivery of the same to the Customer) until the price of the Goods comprised in the contract and all other money due from the Customer to the Company on any other account has been paid in full.

c
We shall retain ownership of the .... until you have finished .... for them.

18.2 Match the sentences containing Latin terms (1–7) with the sentences which have similar meaning (a–g). Look at B opposite to help you.

1 There is a prima facie case to answer.
2 They have entered a caveat.
3 Their action was ultra vires.
4 The newspapers cannot report details of the case because it is sub judice.
5 An ex parte application was lodged at the court.
6 The court sat in camera.
7 An ad hoc committee was formed.

a They acted in a way which was beyond their legitimate powers.
b An application for an injunction was made to the court by one party and no notice was given to the other party.
c The case was heard in private, with no members of the public present.
d They have warned us they have an interest in the case, so they will need notice before we take any further steps.
e A committee was set up for the particular purpose of investigating the issue.
f The action should proceed because one side has shown there seems to be sufficient evidence.
g The case cannot be mentioned in the media if it is likely to prejudice court proceedings.

Over to you

What are the advantages and disadvantages of drafting legal text in 'plain' language?

For information on the plain English movement, go to: www.plainenglish.co.uk/law.htm

19 Business organisations

A Sole trader

Jamie Anderson, a partner in the commercial department of a law firm, is commenting on the choices for different **trading vehicles** for business.

'A client wanting to operate a business for profit might select from a number of different **trading entities**. Each has different legal characteristics and is subject to different rules and regulations. The simplest and commonest form of business structure is a **sole trader**. This generally suits a relatively small enterprise, such as an independent software developer, a hairdresser, or a small shop. It's headed by a single individual and it differs from a company in that the ownership and management is usually vested in the same person, who is personally responsible for all the **debts** of the business, and may thus risk becoming **bankrupt**. Finances are confidential and formalities are few, aside from Value Added Tax, or VAT, regulations.'

B Partnerships

'A common form of structure for certain kinds of business, for example accountants, solicitors, and architects, is a **partnership**. This needs to have at least two **members** and normally a maximum of twenty. There is an **exemption** on size for some types of firm, such as solicitors and accountants. All the **partners** may be **jointly and severally liable** for all the debts of the business. The relationship between the partners is usually drafted in the **Partnership Agreement**. This can set out the **duration** of the partnership, its name and business, how profits, losses, and running costs are to be shared, how much **capital** each partner is to contribute, what rules will apply to the capital, what **grounds** will lead to a partner being **expelled from** the company, what restrictions are imposed on partners, and so on. It's also possible to have a **Limited Liability Partnership**, or **LLP**, which has a legal identity separate from its members. In this sense it resembles a limited company (see text C). It's possible for all the partners except one, known as the **general partner**, to be a **limited partner**. A **sleeping partner** may have a share in the business but doesn't work in it. An individual is therefore able to invest capital in an LLP without risking any further liability. LLPs must be registered with the Registrar of Companies.'

C Limited Companies

'A **Private Limited Company (Ltd)** is a separate **legal entity** which can **sue**, and be sued, in its own right. The Company is identified by its registered number, which will remain the same irrespective of any changes of name. A business can start life as a limited company and this may be particularly appropriate where high-risk projects are involved. In some instances, directors will be asked to **guarantee the obligations** of a company, for example by giving **security over personal assets** to guarantee company borrowing. This is particularly common in the case of new companies who are not able to demonstrate a history of profitable trading. A **Public Limited Company**, or **PLC**, is differentiated from a Private Limited Company in that the **shares** can be sold to the general public via the stock market to **raise share capital**. It's mandatory for a PLC to have at least two **shareholders**, two directors, and a professionally qualified **Company Secretary**. The **minimum authorised share capital** is £50,000 and 25% must be paid up. Before the company can trade or borrow money, a **Trading Certificate** has to be obtained from the **Registrar of Companies** (see Unit 20).'

19.1 Match the two parts of the sentences then replace the underlined words and phrases with alternative words and phrases from A and B opposite. There is more than one possibility for one of the underlined phrases.

1 Choosing an appropriate <u>business medium</u> depends on
2 An individual's business will cease to trade if
3 A small enterprise where one person bears the responsibility and takes the profits
4 In an ordinary partnership, all the partners are
5 In a Limited Partnership, a <u>specified</u> partner bears the risk
6 Partners need to decide
7 Details such as the division of profits and losses may be
8 Accountancy firms may have more than twenty members
9 Misconduct by a partner might lead to

a the <u>starting date and length</u> of the partnership.
b for the firm's debts, while limited partners have restricted liability.
c set out in the <u>deeds (formal documents) of the partnership</u>.
d her being <u>forced to leave</u> the partnership.
e because of <u>freedom</u> from the normal provision under the law.
f <u>responsible collectively and individually</u> for the financial losses of the business.
g a court declares the businessman is <u>incapable of paying his debts</u>.
h may be run by a <u>single business person</u>.
i a number of factors, such as the size and type of business and the need to limit liability.

19.2 Make word combinations from C opposite using words from the box. Then use appropriate word combinations to answer the questions below.

Registrar of	Public	authorised capital	over personal assets	minimum
raise	guarantee	Companies	security	share capital
the obligations	entity	legal	Limited Company	

1 In a private limited company, what guarantee may a director have to provide in order to borrow capital?
2 What type of business organisation must have £12,500 of shares paid up?
3 Which official keeps a record of all incorporated companies, the details of their directors and their financial states?
4 It is mandatory for a PLC to have 25% of what paid up?
5 What is the purpose of a PLC selling shares to the public?

A sole trader

A partnership

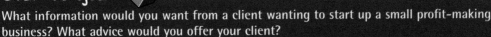

Over to you

What information would you want from a client wanting to start up a small profit-making business? What advice would you offer your client?

For more information on UK company registration, go to: www.companieshouse.gov.uk/.

20 Formation of a company

Incorporation

Jamie Anderson, a partner in the commercial department of a law firm, is discussing the formation of a company in the UK with an overseas client.

'The regulations for **incorporation**, that is, forming a company, are set out in the Companies Act 1985. There are a number of steps to be followed in this procedure. We offer this service to clients, as do accountants and other private sector **formation**, or **registration**, **agents**. Firstly, it's necessary to choose a name for the company which is legally acceptable. The name to be registered isn't necessarily the same as the **trading name**. The application for **registration** will be rejected if the name can't be distinguished easily from a company which already exists as a **registered company**. The use of certain words, for example 'British', 'International' and 'European', may require prior approval before they can be used in a company name. Form 10, which gives the names of the **directors** and **Company Secretary** (see Unit 23), and form 12, are submitted to the **Registrar of Companies** at Companies House in the respective jurisdiction[1]. On completion of registration, the new company will be given a **company number**, also known as a **registered number**, which remains constant throughout its life, and Companies House will issue a **Certificate of Incorporation**. In fact, it's possible to begin trading as a company by purchasing a **shelf company**, which is already registered, and having its **shares transferred**. This is a route chosen by clients where speed is a prerequisite.

A company must have an office in the jurisdiction at which it can be served with any legal process. The **statutory books**, or official company registers, must also be kept there and be available for inspection. Details of any registered company – its **registered office**, company number, **accounting reference date**, date of its financial year end, and history of previous names – can be found free of charge at Companies House.'

[1]For companies registered in England or Wales – Companies House in Cardiff. For companies registered in Scotland – Companies House in Edinburgh.

Memorandum and Articles of Association

'When a company is incorporated, it must adopt **Memorandum and Articles of Association**, also known as the 'Mem and Arts'. The Memorandum sets out the Company's **objects**, or purposes, and it's important to ensure that these properly reflect the company's intentions, for example the ability to **mortgage** company property for the purpose of raising finance. The Articles set out the relationship between the company and its shareholders. The requirements for directors' and shareholders' meetings are also set out here, as are restrictions on share transfer and **allotment of new shares**, and regulations concerning directors' powers and duties. Most companies are **limited** companies with the **liability** of members limited to the nominal value of the shares they hold or, less commonly, the amount they guarantee to contribute to the company's liability on **liquidation** – if the company is closed and its assets sold. A company must have a stated number of **shares issued** to properly identified **shareholders**. Any company will have a maximum amount of **share capital** which can be issued, known as the **authorised share capital**. A company need not issue all its authorised share capital.'

> BrE: Articles of Association; AmE: Bylaws
> BrE: Memorandum of Articles of Association; AmE: Articles of Incorporation

Note: For more information about shares, see Unit 21.

20.1 Jamie's client has sent an email asking more about shelf companies. Complete Jamie's reply. Look at A opposite to help you. There is more than one possibility for one of the answers.

Send Chat Attach Address Fonts Colours Save As Draft

From: j.anderson@happrewandco.co.uk
To: m.lynch@buchan.co.uk
Subject: A shelf company

Dear Michael,

You enquired about shelf companies. These are companies which are already registered at Companies House – often with a name which is linked to the (1) .... , for example 'XY 1000' where XY is the initials of the solicitor's firm. The shares of the company are (2) .... to the purchaser, who normally urgently requires a (3) .... The (4) .... is usually changed and a new Board of Directors and a (5) .... are appointed to replace the initial Board and Secretary, who resign on transfer. Such companies usually have standard Articles of Association. The purchaser acquires the Certificate of (6) ....

20.2 Jamie shows his client a sample Memorandum. Replace the underlined words and phrases with appropriate legal terms from A and B opposite.

No. of Company SC125543
The Companies Act 1985
PRIVATE COMPANY (1) <u>RESTRICTED</u> BY SHARES
MEMORANDUM AND (2) <u>REGULATIONS</u> OF ASSOCIATION
LANCELOT LIMITED

(Incorporated the 29th day of May 2002)
Arthur Evans Ltd, Registration Agents, 1 Tantallon Street, Edinburgh
1. The Name of the Company is "LANCELOT LIMITED".
2. The Company's (3) <u>location</u> is to be situated in Scotland.
3. The Company's (4) <u>purposes</u> are:–
   (a) To carry on for profit, directly or indirectly, whether by itself or through subsidiary, associated or allied companies or firms in the United Kingdom or elsewhere in all or any of its branches any business, undertaking, project or enterprise of any description whether of a private or public character and all or any trades, processes and activities connected therewith or ancillary or complementary thereto.
   (b) To carry on any other trade or business whatever which can in the opinion of the Board of Directors be advantageously carried on in connection with or ancillary to any of the businesses in the Company.
   (c) To purchase or by any other means acquire and take options over any property whatever, and any rights or privileges of any kind over or in respect of property.

   (f) To improve, manage, construct, repair, develop, exchange, let on lease or otherwise (5) <u>borrow capital with property as security</u>, charge, sell, dispose of, turn to account, grant licences, options, rights and privileges in respect of, or otherwise deal with all or any part of the property and rights of the Company.

   (y) To do all such things as may be deemed incidental or conducive to the attainment of the Company's objects or any of them.
4. The (6) <u>responsibility</u> of the members is limited.
5. The Company's share (7) <u>asset value</u> is £10,000 divided into 10,000 shares of £1 each.

Over to you

What procedures are necessary to form a limited company in a jurisdiction you are familiar with?

For information on company formation in the UK, go to: www.companies-house.gov.uk/.

21 Raising capital by share sale

A Share capital

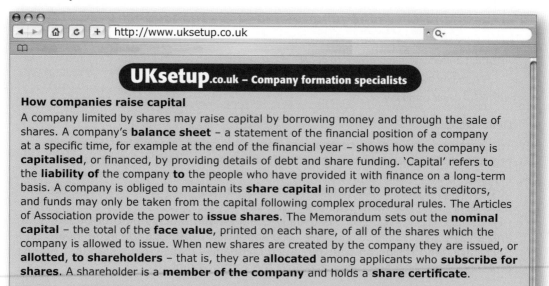

UKsetup.co.uk – Company formation specialists

How companies raise capital

A company limited by shares may raise capital by borrowing money and through the sale of shares. A company's **balance sheet** – a statement of the financial position of a company at a specific time, for example at the end of the financial year – shows how the company is **capitalised**, or financed, by providing details of debt and share funding. 'Capital' refers to the **liability of** the company **to** the people who have provided it with finance on a long-term basis. A company is obliged to maintain its **share capital** in order to protect its creditors, and funds may only be taken from the capital following complex procedural rules. The Articles of Association provide the power to **issue shares**. The Memorandum sets out the **nominal capital** – the total of the **face value**, printed on each share, of all of the shares which the company is allowed to issue. When new shares are created by the company they are issued, or **allotted, to shareholders** – that is, they are **allocated** among applicants who **subscribe for shares**. A shareholder is a **member of the company** and holds a **share certificate**.

B Share value

All shares have a **nominal value**, generally of £1, also known as the **par value**. This value is set out in the capital clause of the Memorandum. Shares can be issued **at a premium** – for a sum greater than their nominal value – but they cannot be issued **at a discount** – less than nominal value. Contracts for the sale of shares may provide for **deferred payment**, that is, part may be left outstanding until the company **makes a call for**, or requests, the unpaid amount. The **market value** of a share depends upon the profitability of the company and the sum of its assets. The legal nature of a share for the shareholder will depend upon the contractual rights attached to the share, which is a **chose in action** – a personal right which can be enforced or claimed as if it were property.

C Rights attaching to shares

A company may issue different **classes** of shares, which have different rights attached to them. The usual rights include:

- A **right to dividend**, that is, a share in the profits. A company may only **declare a dividend** if it has made a profit.
- A right to **vote on resolutions**, for example proposals on matters relating to the approval of directors' contracts, at the company's **annual general meeting (AGM)** – a meeting of all the shareholders with the directors.
- A right to repayment of the investment in the event that the company is **wound up**, or closed.

Other rights are given as a matter of law by the Companies Act 1985. These rights are generally only given to shareholders with voting rights at company meetings. The Act provides that shares must first be offered to shareholders in proportion to their existing **shareholding** on terms at least as favourable as those offered to potential new shareholders. This is the right of **pre-emption**. Members of the company have 21 days in which to **exercise the right**. It does not apply if shares are issued for a **non-cash consideration**, that is, the price, not necessarily money, paid in exchange for the shares.

21.1 Match the two parts of the sentences then replace the underlined words and phrases with alternative words and phrases from A opposite. Pay attention to the grammatical context. There is more than one possibility for one of the answers.

1 Shares can only be issued
2 The company Articles may allow directors
3 If more shares are applied for than the company has to offer,
4 Someone who owns shares is
5 The ownership of shares is

a the company can <u>divide out</u> the shares.
b known as a <u>shareholder</u>.
c to equal the <u>total face value of all the shares</u> of the company, as set out in the Memorandum of Association.
d generally evidenced by a <u>receipt</u>.
e to raise capital by <u>selling</u> shares.

21.2 Make word combinations from B and C opposite using words from each box. Then use the word combinations to replace the underlined words and phrases in the sentences below.

declare	the right
defer	at a premium
exercise	a resolution
issue	a dividend
vote on	payment

1 The Companies Act requires 75% of the shareholders to <u>show their opinion about</u> a special <u>proposal</u> to change the company Articles.
2 The company will <u>announce publicly</u> that shareholders are going to be paid <u>a proportion of the company's profits</u>.
3 Current holders of shares may <u>use their entitlement</u> to buy newly issued shares before they are offered to new shareholders.
4 You can <u>postpone paying in full</u> for the shares until the company requests the unpaid sum.
5 The company can <u>offer</u> shares <u>for sale at a higher price than their par value</u>.

Share certificates

Share prices

Over to you

What rights do shareholders have in a legal jurisdiction you are familiar with?

For information on shares in the UK, go to the London Stock Exchange: www.londonstockexchange.com/en-gb/.

22 Debt financing: secured lending

A ## Granting security

Usha Patel, a company lawyer, is advising Patsy Nielsen, the director of her client company, Rosie Glow Cosmetics Limited. The client wishes to acquire and equip new business premises which are offered for sale, together with an adjacent unit, for a price of £280,000. W.W.Jones Bank has offered the company a loan of £300,000.

Usha: I see that the bank's **facility letter** makes the loan conditional upon the **grant** of a **debenture** to include a **floating charge over** all the company's **assets**, so, anything of value belonging to the company. There's also a first **legal charge** over the property, which is like a **mortgage**. I suppose that's not surprising given that there's a shortfall, you know, a gap, between the purchase price of the property and the total of the loan. Have you had a **valuation** yet?

Patsy: A **survey** has been done – we're waiting for the report. I actually suspect that the valuation will be slightly higher than the agreed price, because the seller's in financial difficulty and wants a quick sale.

Usha: Well, we'll see what the valuation comes out at. If it's really close to the £300,000, I think we should try to persuade the bank that they'll have adequate **security** without a floating charge over all the assets. As I recall, the company has a pretty high asset value with your existing machinery already. It may be that the bank will agree to go with a debenture which is limited to a charge over the **freehold** – that's your absolute right to hold the property or land without paying rent – and a **fixed charge** over the machinery. Now, the company hasn't **granted** security before. Are you familiar with the concept of charges?

Patsy: Not very.

Usha: Well, if the debenture is granted at the same time as **completion** – that's the final stage in the sale of the property – it'll include a mortgage over the freehold property. This is effectively a **transfer of the title to the property** to the bank as **mortgagee**, subject, of course, to an obligation to transfer it back on **repayment** of the loan. The fixed charge will be over other property interests and will usually include shares, goodwill, book debts, and machinery. This means that in the event of **default**, the charged assets can be **appropriated** by the **charge holder**, who's a **secured creditor**, to be sold in order to recover the sum secured.

B ## The terms of a charge

Usha: The terms of the mortgage and fixed charge will usually contain insurance obligations and restrictions on the company's ability to deal with the **charged assets** without the bank's consent. For instance, if the adjacent unit is surplus to your requirements and you decide to **let** it to a tenant, as the **lessor** you'll need to obtain the bank's consent. This will usually involve them approving the form of **lease**. Assets which are of a more transient nature, such as stock, can't be secured by a fixed charge, so a floating charge can be used. While a floating charge is in place a company can still deal with the assets without the consent of the charge holder. A floating charge is sometimes described as being like a large cup; it hangs inverted above the assets and doesn't affect the **chargor** unless the charge **crystallises**. At this point, it descends upon the assets and becomes a fixed charge. Usually a bank gives notice of **crystallisation**. I imagine the debenture will contain a negative **pledge**, which is a type of undertaking. It means that you won't be able to create any other interest in the charged property, including those subject to the floating charge, without consent.

22.1 Complete the definitions. Look at A opposite to help you.

1 grant .... – agree to secure the changing assets of a company, for example stock, not any specific asset

2 grant .... – agree to secure a particular asset, for example equipment or property

3 grant .... – agree to a document in which a company acknowledges a debt in exchange for security over the company's assets specified in the document

4 grant .... – agree to guarantee repayment of a loan by charging assets or property in favour of the lender

5 grant .... – agree to a document transferring an interest in land or buildings as security for the payment of a debt

22.2 Complete this extract from a law firm's website with words from the box. Look at A opposite to help you.

secured	mortgage	floating charge	debenture	repayment	insolvent
defaults	creditors	charge	charge holder	assets	fixed charge

A company may be funded by a loan, for example from a bank, on which it pays interest and for which repayment may be guaranteed by a (1) .... or a (2) .... on one of the company's (3) .... , for example a building or land owned by the company. This is certified by a document generally called a (4) .... Debenture holders are (5) .... of the company. If the company becomes (6) .... , that is, unable to pay its debts, debenture holders are entitled to priority over non-secured creditors to receive (7) .... Debenture holders are normally (8) .... by a (9) .... over specific property. Assets which are of a more changeable nature, such as vehicles, cannot be secured by a fixed charge, so a (10) .... may be used. If the company (11) .... , its assets may be seized by the secured (12) ....

22.3 Complete the table with words from A and B opposite and related forms. Put a stress mark in front of the stressed syllable in each word. The first one has been done for you. Then complete the definitions below with words from the table.

Noun - type of legal agreement	Noun - legal person who assigns (transfers) an interest or use in a property to another	Noun - legal person who has been assigned an interest in or use of a property
'mortgage	'mortgagor	mortga'gee
	chargor	
grant		
		lessee (tenant)

1 A .... agrees to a charge over their property as a security for a loan.

2 A .... lends money to the mortgagor and has a charge over the mortgagor's property.

3 A .... grants a lease on a property.

Over to you

What types of guarantee are offered as security for loans in your legal system? How can investors discover whether a company has charges over its assets?

23 Company directors and company secretaries

A Qualifications and duties of a company director

http://www.happrewandco.co.uk/international

Happrew &Co | About us | Services | Know-how | People | Fees | Contact/find us | Search | FAQs | For our overseas clients

Company directors

There are no mandatory qualifications to become a director of a private or public limited company (plc), although the following **persons** are **disqualified** and are not allowed to hold the position:

- an **undischarged bankrupt**, who has not been released by the court from his debts, unless **leave**, or permission, is obtained from the court;
- a person disqualified by a court from acting as a company director. If leave is given by a court, it must be for the person to be appointed as a director for a specific company;
- in Scotland, a person under the age of 16;
- anyone over the age of 70 in the case of a plc. This age requirement may be **waived**, or ignored, in the case of a candidate named by a general meeting of the company.

Although incorporation limits liability, the directors retain personal responsibility to ensure the company **complies with** the **filing of documents** at Companies House on time, as required by the Companies Act. Failure to do so is a criminal offence and may result in the imposition of a fine together with a criminal record. Persistent failure to fulfil these duties may lead to **disqualification from holding the office of director** in the future. The directors must ensure that:

- **accounts** for limited companies are **delivered to** the Registrar of Companies **within the requisite period**, normally within ten months of the **accounting reference date** in the case of private limited companies or within seven months in the case of a plc, although the requisite period may be amended by legislation. The **defaulting** company may be charged a **late filing penalty** in addition to any other fine imposed by a court;
- **annual returns** are **submitted** as specified by the Act. In the event that these are not submitted, and the Registrar believes that the company is no longer operating, he may **strike it off the register** and **dissolve** it. Any **assets** of the company at that point may become the **property of the Crown**;
- **notice of change** of directors or their details is **provided to** the Registrar;
- notice of any change to the registered office is provided to the Registrar. If this is not done, **statutory notices** may be validly **served on** the registered office.

B Qualifications and duties of a company secretary

Company secretaries

The qualifications required to be a company secretary are set out in the Companies Act 1985. As a company officer, the company secretary may be criminally liable for a **default** committed by the company, for example failure to **file** the company's annual return with Companies House in time. An employment contract will usually specify the **remit** of their duties, that is, the areas of responsibility, which normally include:

- maintaining the statutory registers, for example the register of members;
- filing the **statutory forms**, for example notifying changes among the directors;
- **serving** members and auditors **with** notice of meetings;
- supplying a copy of the accounts to every member of the company;
- keeping **minutes** of directors meetings and general meetings.

23.1 Find answers to the FAQs below. Look at A opposite to help you.

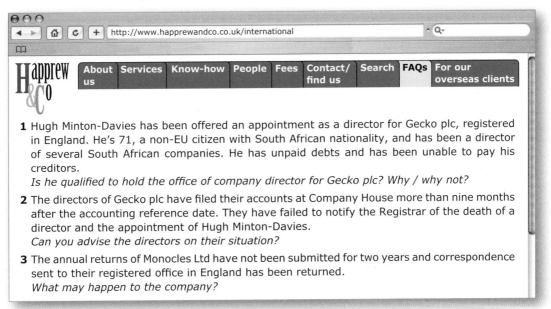

1 Hugh Minton-Davies has been offered an appointment as a director for Gecko plc, registered in England. He's 71, a non-EU citizen with South African nationality, and has been a director of several South African companies. He has unpaid debts and has been unable to pay his creditors.
Is he qualified to hold the office of company director for Gecko plc? Why / why not?

2 The directors of Gecko plc have filed their accounts at Company House more than nine months after the accounting reference date. They have failed to notify the Registrar of the death of a director and the appointment of Hugh Minton-Davies.
Can you advise the directors on their situation?

3 The annual returns of Monocles Ltd have not been submitted for two years and correspondence sent to their registered office in England has been returned.
What may happen to the company?

23.2 A new managing director, Simon Brown, is getting an update from the company secretary, Helen Bernard. Match Simon's questions (1–5) with Helen's responses (a–e). Then replace the underlined words and phrases with alternative words and phrases from A and B opposite. There is more than one possibility for three of the answers.

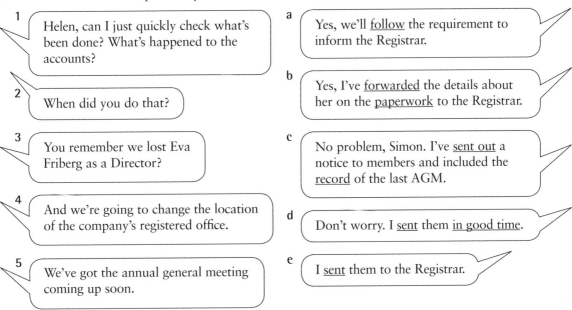

1 Helen, can I just quickly check what's been done? What's happened to the accounts?

2 When did you do that?

3 You remember we lost Eva Friberg as a Director?

4 And we're going to change the location of the company's registered office.

5 We've got the annual general meeting coming up soon.

a Yes, we'll <u>follow</u> the requirement to inform the Registrar.

b Yes, I've <u>forwarded</u> the details about her on the <u>paperwork</u> to the Registrar.

c No problem, Simon. I've <u>sent out</u> a notice to members and included the <u>record</u> of the last AGM.

d Don't worry. I <u>sent</u> them <u>in good time</u>.

e I <u>sent</u> them to the Registrar.

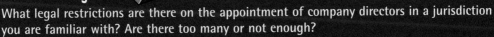

Over to you

What legal restrictions are there on the appointment of company directors in a jurisdiction you are familiar with? Are there too many or not enough?

For more information, go to the Directors and Secretaries Guide in the UK at: www.companieshouse.gov.uk/.

24 Insolvency and winding up

A Insolvency

Charles Stanley, an insolvency lawyer, is advising a client.

'**Insolvency** describes the financial state of a company when its debts or liabilities exceed its assets and available cash. As soon as a company is **insolvent**, it must take action to resolve the situation. This may include renegotiating debt, **realising assets** to **discharge debt**, or even borrowing more money and increasing the liabilities. There's a wealth of legislation that imposes obligations on company officers **in relation to** the interests of creditors. There are **secured creditors**, whose lending is protected by security over the company's assets, for example banks, and there are **unsecured creditors**, often **suppliers**, who may initiate action to achieve repayment. There are also **preferential creditors**, such as the company's own employees, for example in cases where wages haven't been paid, and **occupational pension schemes**. The options available to an insolvent company will be affected by the position taken by its creditors, and the various parties may seek legal advice. My colleagues and I often work **on behalf of** clients with a specialist accountant, an **insolvency practitioner**, also known as an **IP**.'

B Insolvency scenarios

Look at this extract from a leaflet describing possible insolvency scenarios.

Action initiated	Result
A **charge holder** (see Unit 22) – including holders of floating charges created since the Enterprise Act 2002 – or the **company directors file notice at court** for an administration order.	An order is made by the court appointing an **administrator** to take control of the company and to maintain it as a **going concern**. The company is then said to be '**in administration**'.
A charge holder with a floating charge created before the Enterprise Act 2002 appoints an **administrative receiver** (an AR).	The receiver must realise the assets subject to the floating charge on behalf of the charge holder. The floating charge **crystallises** and is **treated as** a fixed charge. Certain creditors will have rights in priority to the charge holder's. A company in administrative receivership is often said to be '**in receivership**'.
A creditor or company directors **petition the court** to make a **winding up** order.	The court makes a winding up order and the company is put into **compulsory liquidation**. A **liquidator** is appointed to realise the company's assets.
Shareholders decide to **put the company into liquidation** when the company is still **solvent**, that is, has sufficient assets to discharge the company's debts.	**Members' voluntary liquidation**
Shareholders decide to put the company into liquidation if the company is insolvent. Creditors accept the liquidator.	**Creditors' voluntary liquidation**
Company directors, **with the assistance of** an authorised insolvency practitioner, apply to the court for approval of a formal arrangement with creditors, as **set out in** a proposal to pay creditors under the supervision of the IP.	**Company voluntary arrangement** (CVA) and appointment of a **supervisor**

24.1 Choose the correct word in brackets to complete the sentences. Look at A opposite to help you.

1 A (debtor/creditor/director) is a person or body owed money by a company.
2 The creditors may take action in relation to a/an (bankrupt/solvent/insolvent) company that will result in the company becoming subject to one of several insolvency regimes.
3 Suppliers are often (unsecured/preferential/secured) creditors.
4 Employees and occupational pension schemes fall within the class of (solvent/preferential/secured) creditors, who are entitled to receive certain payments in priority to secured creditors.
5 A liquidator is appointed by the creditors or the members to (exceed/realise/discharge) assets which may then be divided up among the creditors.
6 If the company has insufficient assets to (discharge/realise/exceed) its debts, creditors may decide to put the company into liquidation.

24.2 Answer the questions. Look at B opposite to help you. There may be more than one possible answer.

1 Who can initiate
  a voluntary liquidation?
  b a company voluntary arrangement?
  c compulsory liquidation?
  d a company going into administration?
2 How can a charge holder obtain an administration order?
3 How may company directors obtain a winding up order?
4 What term describes the stage at which a floating charge descends upon the assets and becomes as though it were a fixed charge?
5 How could you describe a company that is actively trading?
6 What term describes the process of ending the carrying on of a company?
7 What term describes the state of being able to pay all debts or claims?

24.3 Complete this extract from an email about an insolvency proceeding with prepositions from A and B opposite.

Send **Chat** **Attach** **Address** **Fonts** **Colours** **Save As Draft**	

From: chas.stanley@dsbsolicitors.com
To: p.j.s@bedford-lay.com
Subject: J.I.T Ltd

Dear Peter,

Further to our phone discussion, I'm writing (1) .... behalf (2) .... my client whose interest in J.I.T Ltd is set (3) .... in a document I've sent under separate cover. The document was drawn up (4) .... the assistance (5) .... an insolvency specialist and should be treated (6) .... a working draft. Could you let me have your opinion (7) .... relation (8) .... the interests of other creditors and as soon as possible?

Over to you

What happens if insolvency proceedings are instituted against a company in a legal jurisdiction you are familiar with?

For more information about insolvency in the UK, go to the UK insolvency helpline at: www.insolvencyhelpline.co.uk/.

25 Alternative dispute resolution

A Alternative dispute resolution

Anna Chapter heads the Litigation team in a large firm of solicitors. She is talking to a client about **alternative dispute resolution**.

'Alternative dispute resolution, often abbreviated to **ADR**, is well-established in a number of jurisdictions, including the USA, Canada and Australia. Over recent years, we've seen the emergence of **mediation organisations** and **dispute resolvers**, some on the Internet. In the UK, ADR is positively promoted for use in a wide range of civil disputes, including small claims, family matters, construction or building contracts, and complex international commercial disputes. It's generally proposed as a cost-effective alternative to the litigation process and entered into on a voluntary basis by **disputants**, or because of **contractual provisions**, that is, the conditions of a contract. Many commercial **agreements** now include **dispute resolution clauses** in which the **contracting parties** agree the method to be used if a dispute occurs during the life of the contract. However, parties may also **be referred to ADR** by the court during the course of litigation. A Civil Procedure Rule requires the UK civil courts, as part of the case management process, to encourage and facilitate parties to use ADR procedure if appropriate. A National Mediation Helpline has also been set up to provide advice by telephone or online.'

B ADR procedures

ADR refers to a number of different procedures used to **reach a settlement**. Some frequently used methods are:

- **Arbitration** – this is a more formal and binding process where the dispute is **resolved** by the **arbitrator** nominated by both parties.

- **Mediation** – possibly the most popular process. An independent **third party**, normally with appropriate expertise in the area of **contention** or dispute, is appointed by the parties to act as a **mediator**. The mediation process begins with an all parties discussion; following this the respective parties separate to discuss the issues and, with the assistance of the mediator, seek to negotiate a settlement. If settlement is reached, it can become a legally binding contract.

- **Med-Arb** – the dispute is initially submitted to mediation but if **mediated settlement** cannot be reached, then the matter is referred to arbitration.

- **Adjudication** – the method most commonly used in construction disputes. A quick decision is made by the **adjudicator** and a time period is specified during which either party may give notice to refer the matter to arbitration or litigation. The adjudicator's decision is **binding upon** the parties and must be followed, unless and until a later decision is made by an arbitrator or the court.

25.1 Complete the table with words from A and B opposite and related forms. Put a stress mark in front of the stressed syllable in each word. The first one has been done for you.

Verb	Noun – concept or object	Noun – person	Adjective
re'fer	re'ferral		
dispute			
resolve			
		contractor	

25.2 Complete the extract from a model ADR clause with words from the table above and A opposite. Pay attention to the grammatical context.

> 1. Dispute Resolution Procedure
>
> 1.1 **General**
>
> 1.1.1 All disputes between the (1) .... arising out of or relating to this Agreement shall be referred, by either (2) .... , to the project board for resolution.
>
> 1.1.2 If any dispute cannot be (3) .... by the project board within a maximum of 114 days after it has been referred under Clause 1.1.1, that (4) .... shall be (5) .... to the [*appropriate officer*] of the [*public sector client*] and the [*e.g. project manager*] of the (6) .... for resolution.
>
> 1.1.3 Work and activity to be carried out under this (7) .... shall not cease or be delayed by this dispute (8) .... procedure.

25.3 Complete the extract from an email about online ADR using words from the table above and A and B opposite. Pay attention to the grammatical context.

> Tom – there's been some client interest in online ADR. Settlement websites in the US are offering a mediation service on the basis of an agreed (1) .... by the parties. Some organisations are experimenting with chat rooms, creating virtual (2) .... rooms as a way of reducing the costs of resolving disputes. Each party communicates through the online (3) .... via email, who passes responses between the parties. Some websites offer a computer-assisted method for (4) .... disputes over claims. The software compares offers and counteroffers, keeps offers confidential, and pronounces a (5) .... at the mid-point between the defendant's offer and the claimant's demand.

25.4 Are the following statements true or false? Find reasons for your answers in B opposite and the email above.

1 Online mediation is a formal and binding process.
2 The adjudicator passes email responses between parties online.
3 Online mediation is commonly used to resolve construction disputes.
4 The defendant and the claimant are independent third parties.

Over to you

What experience have you had of ADR? Is it supported in a jurisdiction you are familiar with? How? What are the advantages and disadvantages of online mediation?

For more information, look at the Office of Government Commerce at: www.ogc.gov.uk/ and the Centre for Effective Dispute Resolution at: www.cedr.co.uk/.

26 Corporation Tax

Corporation Tax liability in the UK

Corporation Tax is the tax payable on a company's **income** (for example from investment in shares) or **gains** (for example from the sale of assets) at the statutory rate. In this context 'company' is used to refer to the following, in addition to the more conventional meaning of the word:

- **Members' clubs, societies** and **associations** who might have trading activities or income from non-members, for example amateur sports clubs

- **Trade associations,** for example the Association of British Travel Agents (ABTA), the regulatory body for British travel agents

- **Housing associations** – in the UK, independent, not-for-profit bodies that provide low cost 'social housing' for people in housing need

- Groups of individuals carrying on a business, for example **cooperatives**, but not **partnerships** (see Unit 19)

All companies resident in the UK are **subject to** Corporation Tax on their **profits** in an accounting period. A non-UK incorporated company may also be subject to Corporation Tax, if it is managed and controlled from within the UK.

Although Companies House **notifies** the Inland Revenue – the UK tax authority – of the formation of a company on completion of registration, it is still the responsibility of the company to inform the Revenue of its existence and liability to pay tax. This must be done within 12 months of the end of the company's accounting period. An **accounting period** starts when a company first becomes chargeable to Corporation Tax or when the previous accounting period ends. It cannot **exceed** 12 months for the purpose of tax. The normal **due date** for the payment of tax is no later than nine months plus one day after the end of the accounting period, although large companies – that is, those with annual profits **in excess of** a **stipulated amount** – are obliged to pay their tax early by Quarterly **Instalment** Payments.

Word combinations with 'tax'

tax	avoidance	trying legally to minimise the tax to be paid, for example by using **tax loopholes** (gaps in the law)
	benefits	advantages
	bill	demand for money owed in taxes
	chargeable	tax that may be levied on profits
	due	tax that has to be paid by a required date
	efficiency	ways of reducing taxes owed
	evasion	illegally trying to not pay tax
	exemption	a principle permitting freedom from payment of tax. For example, non-profit-making organisations may **claim tax exemption.**
	point	date at which a tax begins to be applied
	relief	help, allowing a company (or individual) not to pay tax on part of their income
	Tax Return	form issued by the taxation authorities for declaration of income and allowances, also known as a **declaration**

26.1 Replace the underlined words and phrases with alternative words from A opposite. Pay attention to the grammatical context. There is more than one possibility for one of the answers.

1 Will you <u>formally inform</u> the Inland Revenue?
2 I believe it's a <u>business run by a group of owners who share the profits and the work</u>.
3 The figure <u>named</u> is currently £1.5 million.
4 We're going to be taxed on <u>money received from sales of goods or services after costs have been deducted</u>.
5 How long have we got until the <u>day on which payment is required</u>?
6 There'll be some tax on <u>money from sale of assets</u> this year.
7 Don't forget, you'll have to pay tax by <u>payment of part of the total sum due</u>.
8 I don't think there'll be much tax on <u>money from investments</u> in this accounting period.
9 Profits aren't going to <u>be greater than</u> £1 million this year.

26.2 Complete this extract from an advisory email from a solicitor with word combinations from B opposite. Use each combination only once.

Send Chat Attach Address Fonts Colours Save As Draft

From: L.Dean@oldfieldslaw.co.uk

To: Bertil.Arvidsson@arbogasystem.se

Subject: UK tax liability

Dear Bertil,

In answer to your query about UK tax liability, I've set out a brief outline below.

The responsibility for the calculation of the tax due lies with the company. Tax is generally (1) .... on the company's total profits – including chargeable gains. A company must follow the special rules in calculating the tax due and, following this self-assessment, submit a Company Tax (2) .... to the Inland Revenue together with the payment of tax (3) ....

If there has been expenditure on research and development, companies may qualify for special tax (4) .... on part of their income. Although there is no annual tax (5) .... for capital gains, roll-over relief may be available where business assets are replaced and trading losses are normally set against income and gains of the same accounting period or even of the previous year. The rules setting out these reliefs and others are complex, and companies generally employ specialist advisers to help maximise their use of the various reliefs in order to minimise their tax (6) ....

The fact that corporate tax rates in the UK are lower than Income tax rates (to which individuals are subject), and that company dividends (which the owners of a company can pay to themselves) are taxed more lightly than other forms of income, means that businesses may opt to incorporate primarily to enjoy such tax (7) .... Again, specialist advice may be sought by non-incorporated businesses that wish to calculate the tax (8) .... of such an option.

Over to you

How is a corporation's taxable income assessed in a jurisdiction you are familiar with? What tax benefits are available to corporations?

For more information on Corporation Tax in the UK, go to HM Revenue and Customs at: www.hmrc.gov.uk/.

27 Mergers and acquisitions

A Mergers and acquisitions

Steve Jakes is a senior partner in a law firm and specialises in **mergers** and **acquisitions**. He's talking to a client from Japan.

'A merger or **takeover** occurs when one company has **acquired** the majority, or even the entirety, of the shares of the **target company**. Statutory schemes of arrangement of companies are contained within the Companies Act. In the conventional non-statutory situation, the **acquiring company**, or **offeror**, usually makes an offer to acquire the shares of the target company, the **offeree**, and gives the shareholders a fixed time within which to accept the offer. The offer is made **subject to the condition** that it will be only be effective in the event that a specified percentage of the shareholders **accept the offer**. The price offered for the shares is usually more than would ordinarily be obtained at that point in time for those shares on the stock market. This constitutes the **takeover bid**. Of course, if the board of directors doesn't recommend the offer to its shareholders, it's regarded as a **hostile takeover**.

The London Stock Exchange

The freedom of companies to **merge** in this way is controlled by various statutes, European Community (EC) **competition authorities** (known as **antitrust regulators** in the US), and the courts, which **regulate anti-competitive concentrations** of market power. If a merger is permitted, **clearance** is **given** by the **regulatory authorities**.'

B Dealing disclosure requirements

'The conduct of takeovers is controlled by rules set by the City Code on Takeovers and Mergers. The Code is administered by the Panel of Takeovers and Mergers, an independent body which draws its members from major financial and business institutions. UK registered and resident public companies have to **abide by** the Code. Disciplinary action may result from certain breaches of the Code, for example failing to **disclose dealings** in **relevant securities** of the offeree company. The **guiding principles** behind the Code are that shareholders are treated fairly and are not denied an opportunity to decide on the merits of a takeover, and that shareholders of the same class are afforded equivalent treatment by an offeror.'

27.1 Complete the table with words from A opposite and related forms. Put a stress mark in front of the stressed syllable in each word. The first one has been done for you.

Verb	Noun	Adjective
a'cquire	acqui'sition	
compete		
regulate		

27.2 Complete the article with words from the table above and A opposite. Pay attention to the grammatical context. There is more than one possibility for one of the answers.

Linde offers £138m to ease delay in BOC bid

Linde has offered to pay BOC Group shareholders up to £138.4 million in compensation if anti-trust (1) .... delay the German group's (2) .... approach. In a move designed to allay fears that regulators could block Linde's £8.2 billion (3) .... for BOC, the German suitor said that it would pay up to 27p per BOC share if it had not received (4) .... clearance in Europe and America by July 26. The cash promise is supposed to partly cover the interim dividend that BOC shareholders would have otherwise received around July or August if their company had remained independent. Neither Linde nor BOC expect (5) .... objections to their proposed (6) .... , although they have given warning that the deal is unlikely to be completed until late summer. They expect regulators to sign off on the deal by the end of May.

The Times

27.3 Steve Jakes is answering a client's enquiry about the rules on dealing disclosure. Complete this extract from his email. Look at A and B opposite to help you. Pay attention to the grammatical context.

Dear Jan,

You asked about dealing disclosure rules in takeovers. Below is a summary of rule 8.3 of the City Code on Takeovers and Mergers, which everyone must (1) .... or risk disciplinary action.

'Under the provisions of Rule 8.3 of the City Code on Takeovers and Mergers (the "Code"), if any person is, or becomes, "interested" (directly or indirectly) in 1% or more of any class of "relevant securities" of [*the offeror* or of] *the* (2) .... *company*, all "dealings" in any "(3) ...." of that company (including by means of an option in respect of, or a derivative referenced to, any such "relevant securities") must be publicly (4) .... by no later than 3.30 pm (London time) on the London business day following the date of the relevant transaction. This requirement will continue until the date on which the (5) .... becomes, or is declared, unconditional as to acceptances, lapses or is otherwise withdrawn or on which the "offer period" otherwise ends. If two or more persons act together pursuant to an agreement or understanding, whether formal or informal, to acquire an "interest" in "relevant securities" of [*the* (6) .... or] *the offeree company*, they will be deemed to be a single person for the purpose of Rule 8.3.'

Over to you

How are shareholders' interests protected during takeovers in a jurisdiction you are familiar with? In your opinion, are takeovers adequately regulated, over regulated or under regulated?

For information on takeovers in the UK, go to: www.thetakeoverpanel.org.uk/.

28 Anti-competitive behaviour

A Competition law

The Competition Act follows Articles 81 and 82 of the European Community (EC) Treaty and is part of a body of law known as **competition law**. Competition law regulates **anti-competitive conduct** that **harms** the market, such as excluding new **competitors** and **putting up**, or **erecting, barriers to competition**. It also covers **abuse of a dominant position**, for example by **distorting competition** or by **predatory pricing** – when goods are sold at less than their cost price to cut out **rival** businesses.

> BrE: competition law; AmE: antitrust law
> BrE: abuse of a dominant position; AmE: abuse of monopoly power

B Competition inquiry

Steve Jakes, a UK lawyer, is talking to a client about how **anti-competitive practices** and **agreements** are dealt with.

'The Competition Commission was established by the Competition Act 1998 and its procedures are governed by provisions of the Enterprise Act 2002. Its purposes include carrying out inquiries into anticipated and completed mergers, and **market investigations** which other authorities, most often the government watchdog (the Office of Fair Trading, or OFT) or the Secretary of State, **refer to** the Commission. When a **merger inquiry** or **market investigation reference** – popularly known in the media as a **referral** – is made, the Chairman selects members, including appropriate specialists, to serve on the three to five-person group that will conduct the inquiry. Procedures are in place to ensure that **conflicts of interest** are avoided. An administrative timetable is drawn up for the inquiry and published on the Commission's website. Merger inquiries can take over six months and market investigations up to two years.'

> BrE: anti-competitive practices and agreements; AmE: restraint of trade

C Information gathering, hearings, and remedies

'For inquiries and investigations, information is collected from a range of sources. Parties are **compelled** to submit documents and the Commission can **impose a monetary penalty** for **non-compliance with** its requirements. It **constitutes an offence** to alter, **suppress,** or destroy documents, or to intentionally provide false or **misleading** information. Hearings are normally held privately with one party at a time, although public and joint hearings are possible.

The Commission has **regulatory powers under the Act** to make and implement decisions and decide on **remedies**. Before there can be any **remedial action**, however, the group must reach a two-thirds majority that there is an anti-competitive outcome, such as a substantial reduction in competition resulting from a merger or an **adverse effect** on a market. The final report will contain remedies for implementation through agreed **undertakings** – that is, binding promises – or imposed orders which are monitored by the OFT. Undertakings and orders are **enforceable** in the courts by civil proceedings. Appeals by an **aggrieved party** – one who disagrees with the decision of the Committee – may be made to the Competition Appeal Tribunal.'

28.1 Choose the correct phrase in brackets to complete the sentences. Look at B and C opposite to help you.

1 Not supplying documents requested by a competition inquiry can lead to (enforceable orders / conflicts of interest / a monetary penalty).
2 The inquiry group must reach a majority decision that there has been anti-competitive conduct which has led to (remedial action / an adverse effect / misleading information) on a market.
3 Remedies decided by the Commission can be implemented through (aggrieved parties / agreed undertakings / adverse effect).

28.2 Complete the article. Look at A, B and C opposite to help you. Pay attention to the grammatical context. There is more than one possibility for one of the answers.

Supermarket competition inquiry may break stranglehold of big four

(a) Supermarkets may be forced to sell off development sites and scale back expansion plans after the Office of Fair Trading yesterday signalled a full scale competition (1) .... into the UK's "big four" grocers.

(b) The OFT said supermarkets had driven through price cuts and seemingly improved quality and choice – but there was evidence they had also erected (2)................................ to keep out new players and their move into convenience stores could (3)................................ competition and (4)................................ consumers.

(c) The (5) .... now intends to (6) .... the big four – Tesco, Asda, Sainsburys and Morrisons – for a Competition Commission inquiry which could last two years. The four chains account for nearly 75% of the £95bn UK grocery market, with Tesco speaking for more than 30%.

(d) The OFT highlighted several areas of concern, including the way supermarkets sell nearly 3,000 popular products at below cost price and use local price cuts and promotions to put pressure on smaller (7)................................ . It also focused on the stores' increasing buying power, which they can use to drive down the prices paid to suppliers.

(e) The OFT also wants a full (8)................................ into the grocers' "landbanks". The supermarkets have acquired hundreds of development sites, many of which, the OFT said, may have been acquired solely to prevent a rival opening a store.

(f) The (9) .... to the commission is a victory for small shopkeepers, who have led the campaign for an inquiry into the big four's domination. The decision represents a U-turn from last summer, when the OFT said there were no grounds for a competition inquiry.

(g) Yesterday OFT chief executive John Fingleton said he had fresh evidence of (10) .... concerns, uncovered by new (11) .... the Enterprise Act 2002, which (12) .... the supermarkets to hand over documents.

The Guardian

28.3 Which paragraphs (a–g) from the article above allege evidence of:

1 predatory pricing?
2 anti-competitive conduct? (two paragraphs)
3 abuse of a dominant position? (two paragraphs)

Look at A opposite to help you.

Over to you

What procedures are in place to check anti-competitive conduct in a jurisdiction you are familiar with? How effective are they? Describe a recent case as if to a foreign colleague.

For information on UK competition law, go to: www.competition-commission.org.uk/ and www.oft.gov.uk/. For information on EU competition policy, go to: http://ec.europa.eu/comm/competition/index_en.html

29 Tort 1: personal injury claim

A Tort

A **tort** is a **civil**, not criminal, **wrong**, which excludes breach of contract. A tort entitles a person **injured by damage or loss** resulting from the tort to **claim damages in compensation**. Tort law has been built upon decisions made in reported court cases. Torts include, for example:

- **negligence** – the **breach of a duty of care** which is **owed to** a **claimant**, who in consequence **suffers injury** or **(a) loss**;

- **trespass** – **direct and forcible injury**, for example if person A walks over B's land **without lawful justification** or A removes B's goods without permission;

- **defamation** – publishing a statement about someone which lowers the person in the opinion of others. This is known as **libel** when in a permanent form, and **slander** if it is in speech;

- **nuisance** – for example if A acts in a way which prevents B from the **use and enjoyment of** his land.

In the case of **product defects causing damage** or **harm** to consumers, **strict liability**, that is, legal responsibility for damage independent of negligence, is imposed on producers and suppliers by the Consumer Protection Act, which puts into effect a European Union Product Liability Directive.

Note: **claimant** – formerly known as **plaintiff** (England and Wales) and **pursuer** (Scotland)

B Client briefing notes – personal injury claims

One of the clients of a large regional law firm is 'Get Fit', a chain of fitness centres. Below is an extract from draft briefing notes prepared by the law firm, intended to inform the managers of 'Get Fit' of the potential cost in the event of a successful **personal injury claim in negligence** following an accident at one of their centres.

A person who has **sustained an injury** at the centre and who believes that they may have a **claim against** the company ('Get Fit') will usually seek advice to assess whether the likely level of damages, i.e. the financial compensation that may be awarded, is sufficient to **justify the risk** of **pursuing a claim**.

The amount of damages, known as the **quantum**, is usually made up of two aspects.

- **General Damages** are paid to **compensate the claimant**, that is, the person making the claim, for the **pain and suffering** resulting from the injury and for the effect this has on their life. These damages are difficult to assess and guidelines are published by the Judicial Studies Board. You may hear these being referred to as the JSB guidelines. Reference is also made to the level of **damages awarded** by courts in similar cases.

- **Special Damages** are calculated more objectively as these consist of claims for the past and future **financial loss** to the claimant. This typically includes **loss of earnings**, in addition to the cost of care and necessary equipment required **as a result of** the injury.

In some cases, when **liability** is **admitted**, it may be appropriate to **make interim payments** on account of the full award. For instance, the claimant may be **undergoing** a course of **medical treatment**. This will fall into the special damages category and payment can therefore be made before the **final claim** is **settled**.

29.1 Complete the definitions. Look at A opposite to help you. There is more than one possibility for one of the answers.

1 .... – a breach of duty towards other people generally
2 .... – financial compensation for loss or injury
3 .... – physical or economic harm or loss
4 .... – person who makes a claim
5 .... – making public a statement which harms someone's reputation
6 .... – total legal responsibility for an offence which has been committed
7 .... – an interference with private property
8 .... – spoken statement which damages someone's character

29.2 Complete the table with words from A and B opposite and related forms. Put a stress mark in front of the stressed syllable in each word. The first one has been done for you.

Noun	Adjective
'slander	'slanderous
defamation	
libel	
liability	
injury	

29.3 Complete this letter regarding a personal injury claim at a 'Get Fit' fitness centre. Look at A and B opposite to help you. Pay attention to the grammatical context. There is more than one possibility for three of the answers.

Dear Sirs

Our client: Ms Paula Kosmaczewski

Re: Accident at Rothbury 'Get Fit' fitness centre on 8 March 2007

We are instructed by the above-named client with regard to a personal (1) .... that took place as a result of an accident in your Rothbury fitness centre on 8 March.

We are instructed that the circumstances of the accident were that our client was running on an exercise machine when the rotating track stopped abruptly and she fell forward and (2) .... an injury to both her right shoulder and right knee. A member of the centre's staff was summoned by another centre user. The staff member assisted our client. Another member of staff said that the running machine had not been maintained recently. Our client was assisted by centre staff to a taxi and went home. On the 30 March our client consulted her doctor because of the pain and restricted movement in her shoulder and knee as a result of the accident. Her doctor referred her to the hospital for specialist examination and treatment. Our client is still (3) .... medical treatment and has recovered 80% but is advised by medical consultants that she is unlikely to recover 100%.

Our client is self-employed as a freelance musician. As a result of the accident she was unable to fulfil ten weeks of contracted work and has (4) .... a loss of (5) ....

As you are aware, under section 2 of the Occupiers' Liability Act 1957 the occupier of the premises (6) .... a duty of (7) .... to all visitors to keep the premises and equipment reasonably safe. Our client's accident results from a failure to keep equipment safe and a member of staff (8) .... liability. Our client has a valid (9) .... against you in (10) ....

Over to you

Describe the liability of a client who owns a leisure or sports centre to users of the centre in a jurisdiction you are familiar with, as if to a colleague from a different legal jurisdiction.

30 Tort 2: clinical negligence

A Clinical negligence practice

David Jones specialises in **clinical negligence** at a regional firm, Jameson's. Katrina MacLellan is a 3rd year law student who is undertaking a summer work placement in the **litigation department** at Jameson's. David is describing his practice to Katrina.

David: At Jameson's, **claimants instruct** us, that is to say, individuals come to us, to get an idea of whether they have a **potential claim**, to find out how strong, their claim is, and what the process will involve. Depending on that advice, they may then instruct us to **pursue the claim** on their behalf. The **likely amount** of **damages** has to be enough to cover the cost of investigating a claim.

Katrina: How do individuals finance this legal work? Isn't it very expensive?

David: Yes, it can be. I'm always very careful to **give** clients **a fee estimate at the outset**. Initially this will just be for the cost of **exploring the claim**. This will involve **obtaining** the client's **medical records** from the relevant general medical practice or hospital. I usually go through these before **instructing an independent expert** to **prepare a report**. The department **keeps a register of experts** which we use for an **impartial**, that is, unbiased, **opinion**. Some clients may have **legal expenses insurance** or may qualify for Public Funding and others may have to fund themselves. In those cases we usually **agree a payment schedule** with the client. If we do pursue the claim this is usually **on a conditional fee basis**, that is, 'no win no fee', so there is an element of risk involved.

Katrina: What does the success of a claim depend on?

David: Well, obviously the basis is that the claimant has **sought medical advice** or **treatment** and believes that as a result of that advice or treatment their health has suffered. We have to show that there is a **causal link** between the two things – that there is **causation**.

The **second essential leg** is that there has been an **element of negligence**. Sometimes this involves extremely complicated evidence. Basically, we need to demonstrate that the course of action or advice given by the doctor **in the case in point** would not be that advised by a similarly experienced and **reputable** body of practitioners. As you can imagine, the role of the expert in all of this is extremely important. We rely upon them to explain how the action of the defendant has **adversely affected the outcome** for the patient.

The other extremely important point is that the claimant must **bring the claim within the limitation period**. This is usually within three years of the event, although this may be extended if the case involves a child or the claimant has a mental disability.

> BrE: conditional fee basis; AmE: contingency fee basis

30.1 Replace the underlined words and phrases with alternative words and phrases from A opposite. There is more than one possibility for three of the answers.

1 We have to decide whether there is a <u>possible case</u>.
2 Has the treatment <u>negatively</u> influenced the health of the client?
3 We look for someone who can give an <u>unprejudiced point of view</u>.
4 It's essential that we're able to establish <u>a connection</u> between treatment and the negative effect upon the client.
5 Once the case has been explored we decide whether to <u>start an action</u>.
6 We have to estimate the <u>probable</u> costs of the action.
7 Clinical negligence cases may be charged to clients <u>in proportion to the damages recovered</u>.
8 <u>In this instance</u>, the claim would be within the limitation period.

30.2 Complete the sentences with verbs from A opposite. Pay attention to the grammatical context.

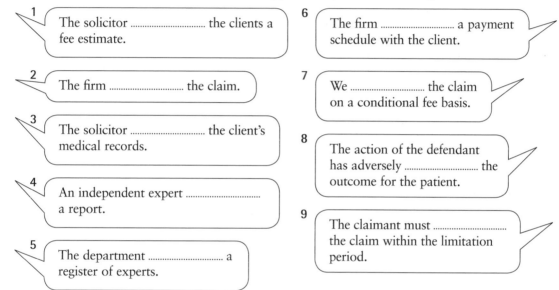

1 The solicitor .... the clients a fee estimate.

2 The firm .... the claim.

3 The solicitor .... the client's medical records.

4 An independent expert .... a report.

5 The department .... a register of experts.

6 The firm .... a payment schedule with the client.

7 We .... the claim on a conditional fee basis.

8 The action of the defendant has adversely .... the outcome for the patient.

9 The claimant must .... the claim within the limitation period.

30.3 Change the spoken statements in 30.2 to passive forms more typical of formal written English, when the focus is on the actions and processes rather than the human agent. The first one has been done for you.

1 <u>The clients are given a fee estimate by the solicitor.</u>
2 ....
3 ....
4 ....
5 ....
6 ....
7 ....
8 ....
9 ....

Over to you

How would you advise a foreign client in English who claims that their health has suffered because of medical treatment in a jurisdiction you are familiar with?

31 Forming a contract 1

A Basic principles

The basic principles of contract law in the English system arise from established custom and rules and are fundamental to all areas of law in practice. Reference is made to these principles in **drafting** and **interpreting the provisions** of any **legal agreement,** such as a **lease,** a **loan agreement,** a **sales agreement,** a **consultancy agreement,** a **hire purchase agreement,** a **hire contract,** or a **service contract,** etc. The principles of contract law will determine whether and at what point a **binding agreement** has been **made** between the **parties concerned.**

Note: The words **contract** and **agreement** are interchangeable in the examples above. For example, a loan agreement / loan contract.

B Formation of a contract

Formation of a contract requires the presence of four essential **elements:**

- **Offer**
  The contract must contain the basic **terms of the agreement** and be **capable of acceptance** without further negotiation. This does not mean that the initial communication between parties will in itself **constitute an offer.** For example, in an **auction** situation, the seller, known as the vendor, may **make an invitation to treat** – invite an offer – by setting out the **conditions of sale** (for example when payment will be made) with the exception of the price. The **offer** is **submitted** by the purchaser, who offers to purchase at a specified price and will usually **incorporate the terms** of the invitation to treat into his/her offer.

- **Acceptance**
  There must be an **unqualified agreement** to proceed on the basis set out in the offer and it must be **communicated to the offeror** – the person making the offer – in order to be effective. If the **offeree** – the person receiving the offer – states that he or she **accepts the offer subject to contract,** that is, some variation of the terms, then **no contract is formed.** This would be a **qualified acceptance,** which constitutes a **counter offer.**

  Issues may arise as to whether the **acceptance** has been **communicated.** Two rules determine this:

  - The **reception rule** applies to **instantaneous** forms of communication, for example telephone calls. The contract is said to be formed when the **acceptance is received by the offeror.**

  - The **postal acceptance rule,** where there is a delay between the communication being sent and received, for example by post. The contract is formed when the **acceptance is sent by the offeree.**

  To **avoid uncertainty,** the offeror may specify the method and timing of acceptance. Agreement on **essential terms,** for example price and delivery, must be certain and not **vague.**

- **Consideration**
  For a contract to be **enforceable** something of value must be given, for example a price, even if it is of **nominal value,** say £1.

- **Intention**
  It is assumed that **contracting parties** intend to **create legal relations,** particularly in commercial circumstances. This is, however, a **rebuttal presumption** – an assumption that can be contradicted – if there is contrary evidence.

31.1 Complete the conversations with the correct legal agreement from A opposite.

> We rented a car for a week in Austria.

> What did the (1) .... cover?

> The office's windows are always dirty. I want them cleaned regularly by a firm of window cleaners.

> You'll need a good (2) ....

> I want to buy a new car but we can't afford to pay the whole price at once. I'm going to pay in monthly instalments.

> You'll need to check the interest rate on the (3) ....

> We're going to be living in London for about 18 months, so we're going to rent a flat.

> Make sure you get a reasonable (4) ....

> I'm going to have to borrow a large sum of money for about three years.

> Try to get the best (5) .... you can from your bank.

31.2 Make word combinations from B opposite using words from the box.

contrary	offer	conditions of	avoid	sale	qualified
parties	essential	contracting	terms	contract	acceptance
counter	uncertainty	evidence	subject to	rebuttal	presumption

31.3 Find answers to these FAQs from a law firm's website. Find reasons for your answers in B opposite.

> 1 Building work started on a major construction project before all the elements of the contract had been agreed. Both parties expected that reaching an agreement would not be a problem. However, final agreement was never reached and eventually the claimants stopped work and claimed for work done. The defendants counter-claimed for the breach (break) in the contract.
> **Under English law, was there a contract?**
>
> 2 Helena applied for shares in a company. The shares were allotted to her and a notice of allotment was posted to her. It never arrived.
> **Under English law, had she become a shareholder or not?**
>
> 3 Two women went regularly to bingo sessions together and had an arrangement to share whatever they won. One of them won a bonanza (extra) prize of £1,107. She claimed it was not covered by the sharing arrangement.
> **Under English law, was their agreement legally binding?**

Over to you

What would be the answers to the questions above in a legal system you are familiar with? What other legal issues might arise? What are the basic elements of a contract in a jurisdiction you are familiar with?

To look at a recent law report on a contract dispute concerning offer and acceptance, see: Pickfords Ltd v Celestica Ltd [2003] EWCA Civ 1741 at: www.bailii.org/databases.html

32 Forming a contract 2

A Form of contract

A **binding contract** must be:

- in the **form required by the law**;
- between parties **with the capacity to contract** – that is, legally capable to contract – or made by agents or representatives of the **contracting parties** with the **authority to act**.

It should be:

- **enforceable** in the event that one of the contracting parties fails to **perform the contract**.

It may be:

- **made in writing**;
- **made orally**;
- **implied from conduct**, that is, by the behaviour of the contracting parties.

However, the law does require that some agreements are made in writing. This is usually because registration is required for the **agreement to be effective** and the relevant registry requires a written agreement. Examples of agreements to be made in writing include:

- contracts for the sale of land;
- contracts of guarantee;
- contracts for transfer of shares;
- contracts which must be made by deed, for example a lease for more than three years.

A **simple contract** requires **consideration** – the price in exchange for a promise to do something – and becomes **effective on execution**, generally when it is signed. In contrast, a **contract by deed** does not require consideration. A deed has different **formal execution requirements** depending on the contracting parties. For example, a deed may need to be **affixed with a seal** – a printed company stamp – if one party is a limited company. Common law requires that a **deed is delivered**. This determines the date from which the **parties are bound**. It must be clear on the face of a deed that it is **executed by the parties as a deed**. Deeds may contain **standard wording** about execution, for example:

> This document is executed as a deed and is delivered and **has effect** at the date written at the beginning of it.

B Void or voidable or unenforceable contracts

Sometimes a contract may be **defective** and may consequently be **void** or **voidable** or **unenforceable**.

A contract may be void – that is, no contract exists – if one, or both, of the parties is not **recognised in law** as having legal **capacity to consent to** a contract, for example **minors** – young people under 18 – or persons with certified mental incapacity.

A contract is **voidable**, that is, it may be **avoided**, or cancelled, by one of the parties if there is some **defect** in its formation. For example, if the contract for the sale of land is not in writing, the parties can either ignore the defect and **treat the contract as fully binding,** or one of the parties can use the defect as a means for **setting the contract aside**.

Some contracts may be neither void nor voidable but cannot be **enforced** in a court of law, for example payment of a gambling debt. **Lapse of time** may **render a contract unenforceable**. The **limitation period** for a legal **action brought under a deed** is usually 12 years from the **date of occurrence of the cause of action**. An action on a simple contract is **barred from** being raised after six years.

32.1 Replace the underlined words and phrases in a solicitor's conversation with his client with alternative words and phrases from A opposite. Pay attention to the grammatical context. There is more than one possibility for two of the answers.

Solicitor: Does she have the (1) <u>power</u> to act as his agent in this agreement?
Client: Yes, she's acting on his behalf.
Solicitor: You understand that you can't rely on an oral agreement. The contract needs to be (2) <u>on paper</u>. When do you want the contract to (3) <u>come into operation</u>?
Client: They want the deed (4) <u>signed, sealed and delivered</u> by 31 July. We've had some problems in the past with suppliers letting us down. Can you make sure this contract will be (5) <u>binding</u>?
Solicitor: We'll use a (6) <u>recognised set of words</u> stating that the provisions are legally binding in the agreement we draw up for you.

32.2 Complete the sentences with words from the box. Look at A and B opposite to help you.

barred	delivered	performed	required	bound	enforced	recognised
brought	executed	rendered	treated	consented	implied	set aside

1 The contract was .... unenforceable after 12 years.
2 The contract was technically voidable but the parties .... it as binding.
3 Because of the limitation period, you are .... from bringing an action.
4 The other party has .... to the terms of the contract.
5 The contract was .... by the court because it was defective.
6 Although there was no written agreement, the court decided the conduct of the parties .... a contract.
7 Registration of the transfer of land is .... by the law.

32.3 Complete the definitions. Look at B opposite to help you.

1 .... – time when an actionable event happened
2 .... – amount of time which is available for someone to start legal proceedings
3 .... – the passing of a period of years

Over to you

What agreements must be made in writing in a jurisdiction you are familiar with? What sort of problems can arise? How are they dealt with?

To look at recent law reports on failure to execute a formal contract, see Bryen & Langley Ltd v Boston [2005] EWCA Civ 973 and Harvey Shopfitters Ltd v ADI Ltd [2003] EWCA Civ 1757 at: www.bailii.org/databases.html

33 Structure of a commercial contract

A Structure of a commercial contract

Most written contracts have a similar structure consisting of certain essential clauses, **irrespective of** the subject matter of the contract. The general pattern of paragraphs can be:

Heading
For example, 'Distribution Agreement'.

Commencement and Date
Usually a commercial contract contains a brief introduction which describes the nature of the agreement, for example 'This Agreement for the sale of …' or 'This Share Agreement …'. The commencement clause will state the date on which the **provisions**, or conditions of the contract, are to **come into effect**. The date is usually inserted in the relevant space **at completion** – the last stage in the formation of a contract.

Parties
The full details of parties are set out. In the case of a company, the registered number is included. This remains unchanged during the life of the company **despite** any changes of name or registered office.

Recitals
Also known as **Background** or **Preamble**. These paragraphs are traditionally introduced by the word **WHEREAS** (conventionally, key words are in capital letters or have an initial capital). The recitals consist of a statement of background facts and the reasons why parties are to **enter into the contract**. Related or **preceding transactions** may be referred to. If a later **dispute** arises **concerning** the operative part, the recitals may be used to **determine construction**, that is, interpret intentions.

Operative provisions
Often introduced by the expression '**The Parties Hereby Agree as follows …**' or similar words, for example '**Whereby it is Agreed as follows …**'. These words signal the start of the operative part of the contract, containing various clauses which **create rights and obligations**, or create and transfer interests in property. Operative provisions in more complex agreements may refer to more detailed **Schedules** (see below).

Definitions
This section states the meaning to be **attributed to** terms essential to the contract – the **defined terms**. Most defined terms are conventionally given capital initial letters, for example Security Documents or Completion Date. **In the absence of** a definition, words within the contract will be given their ordinary and natural meaning.

Interpretation
The aim of this section is to assist in the interpretation and construction of the whole contract by referring to specific uses. There are a number of provisions included in most contracts, for example 'Words **denoting** the singular include the plural meaning and **vice versa**'.

Conditions precedent
These **pre-conditions** must be **satisfied** in order for the agreement, or the relevant parts of it, to come into effect, for example the grant of planning permission. The **conditions precedent clause stipulates**, or imposes, obligations on the relevant party to **procure the satisfaction of the condition** and provide a date by which time the condition precedent must be satisfied. It is usual for an agreement to terminate automatically if this is not achieved by the specified date.

Consideration (see Unit 31)
This sets out the consideration provided by the parties.

Other operative clauses (see Unit 35)
Including, for example, **warranties**, **limitation and exclusion clauses**, and other standard clauses such as governing law.

Schedules
Sections at the end of the contract containing specific provisions and documents, for example the Transfer Deed in a contract for the sale of land.

33.1 Decide which part of a contract described in A opposite these extracts have come from.

1
> "the Schedule"   The Schedule in four Parts annexed and signed as relative to this Agreement.
> "the Buyer"   shall mean the purchaser of the goods from the Company.

2
> The consideration for the sale and purchase of the Contract Shares shall be the net asset value of the Company (subject to…) plus Three hundred and fifty thousand pounds for goodwill subject to adjustment as follows…

3
> WHEREAS the Vendors have agreed to sell to the Purchaser, and the Purchaser has agreed to purchase, the entire issued share capital of Green Boots Limited ("the Company") on the terms set out in this Agreement.

4
> THIS AGREEMENT is made the 1st day of October 2007 BETWEEN Green Boots Limited having its registered office at 104 Warren Court, Beeston, (hereinafter referred to as "the Purchasers" of the first part) and Matching Socks Limited having its registered office at 6 Heel Street, Darnley, (hereinafter referred to as "the Vendors" of the second part).

5
> The masculine includes the feminine and vice versa.

6
> The sale and purchase hereby agreed is conditional upon and subject to the following conditions being satisfied on or before the Completion Date:–
> (i) the Vendors exhibiting to the Purchasers' Solicitors a valid marketable lease in the name of the Company free from any encumbrances to the Property;

7
> The provisions set out in the Fourth Schedule shall have effect and the parties shall undertake their respective obligations as specified therein.

8
> THEREFORE the parties Have Agreed and Hereby CONTRACT AND AGREE as follows:–

33.2 Replace the underlined words and phrases with alternative words and phrases from A opposite. There is more than one possibility for one of the answers.

1 <u>In spite of</u> the differences between the parties at the start of negotiations, their intention was to form an agreement.
2 We, the Parties, <u>in this way</u> agree to purchase the Contract Shares.
3 If a dispute arises <u>with reference to</u> the satisfaction of the pre-conditions, the Purchasers may cancel the agreement.
4 <u>Without</u> the specified documents, the agreement cannot come into effect.
5 Terms denoting masculine references include female and <u>the opposite</u>.

Over to you

What is the typical structure of a commercial contract in a jurisdiction you are familiar with? What sort of standard wordings are used? Are these helpful?

34 Express and implied terms

Express terms

Express terms are **set out** and **stipulated expressly** in the contract. For example:

> The Seller will **within** a period of 6 months from the **date of delivery** of Goods, **where** Goods which are proved to the reasonable satisfaction of both parties to be **damaged** or **defective** or not to comply with the agreed specification **due to defects** in materials or workmanship or to **faulty** design, **repair**, or **at its sole discretion replace**, such Goods, **subject to** the following **conditions**:

A condition is an **essential term of the contract**. If a **condition** is not **performed**, it may constitute a substantial **breach of contract** and allow the other party to **repudiate the contract**, that is, **treat the contract as discharged** or **terminated**. It may also **give rise to a claim for damages**. If all the conditions are performed, the **contract** is **performed**.

A **warranty** is a term which is secondary to the main purpose of the contract. A **breach of warranty** does not in itself permit the other party to treat the contract as discharged, although it may allow the party to **sue for damages** in the event that **loss is suffered**. When deciding whether a party is entitled to repudiate a contract, courts may try to determine the intentions of the parties with regard to the terms. For example, the courts might look at the commercial importance of a term in relation to a particular trade, and examine the seriousness of the consequences of a breach. If statements made by parties before a contract is made are not intended to be legally binding, for example the stated age of an object offered for sale, they are usually known as **representations**. If a representation later **turns out to be** false, this cannot give rise to breach of contract but instead to a possible **action for misrepresentation**.

Implied terms

Implied terms are not **made express** within the contract but may be **implied into the contract** in the following ways:

- **by custom** – a term can only be implied into a contract by custom if there is no express term **to the contrary**. These may be terms which are **customary** in the market in which the contract is made or have been in **previous dealings** between the parties.

- **by statute** – various statutes imply terms into different specific contracts. For example, the condition that employment contracts will be automatically transferred is **implied under statute** in the contract for the sale of a business. In a sale of goods contract there are **implied conditions** that the seller has the right to sell, that the goods correspond with the description, are reasonably fit for the purpose, and are of satisfactory quality. A contract for the lease of a furnished flat automatically contains a specific implied term that the flat be reasonably fit for habitation.

- **by common law** – by the intention of the parties, if it is a term which is necessary to make the contract work.

34.1 Replace the underlined words and phrases in the written contract term below with alternative words and phrases from A opposite. Use each word or phrase only once. There is more than one possibility for one of the answers.

> 8.1 (1) <u>In the situation that</u> the Goods have been manufactured by the Seller and are found to be (2) <u>broken or imperfect</u>, the Seller shall (3) <u>mend</u>, or (4) <u>if it chooses to do so</u>, (5) <u>substitute</u> defective Goods free of charge (6) <u>in less than</u> 2 years from the (7) <u>time the goods are received</u>, (8) <u>depending on</u> the following (9) <u>terms</u>:
>
> 8.1.1 the Buyer notifying the Seller in writing immediately upon the (10) <u>faults</u> becoming apparent;
>
> 8.1.2 the defect being (11) <u>because of</u> the (12) <u>incorrect</u> design, materials or workmanship of the Seller;

34.2 Complete the definitions. Look at A opposite to help you. There is more than one possibility for one of the answers.

1 .... – breaking a contractual condition
2 .... – refuse to carry out obligations under a contract because the other party has not kept to the essential terms of the contract
3 .... – end a contract
4 .... – carry out all the terms of a contract

34.3 Complete the table with the appropriate noun form of words taken from A opposite. Put a stress mark in front of the stressed syllable in each word. The first one has been done for you.

Verb	Noun
'stipulate	stipu'lation
perform	
repudiate	
terminate	
discharge	

34.4 All of the verbs in the box above, except one, collocate with *a contract* or *the contract*. Which verb does not? Look at A to help you. Which noun does the odd one out collocate with?

34.5 A solicitor is talking to her assistant about a phone call with a client. Replace the underlined words and phrases with alternative words and phrases from A and B opposite.

> He says the terms of the (1) <u>guarantee</u> have been breached and his business wants to sue for (2) <u>compensation</u>. The contract (3) <u>says</u> that if the goods are found to be defective, they'll be repaired or replaced, and the seller is refusing to do either. Of course, these conditions may also be (4) <u>set out in a law</u>. We'll need to look at the contract to ensure there's no (5) <u>written</u> term (6) <u>saying the opposite</u>. Can you check if his company has had (7) <u>earlier agreements</u> with the seller?

Over to you

What terms may be implied into contracts in a legal system you are familiar with? How do the courts interpret written contract terms in the case of a dispute?

35 Exclusion, limitation and standard clauses

A Exclusion and limitation clauses

Commercial contracts may **seek to exclude liability for** specific categories of **damage** and to **limit liability for breach of contract**. For example:

> 10.2.5 The Company will **be under no liability for** any defect arising or introduced by a Buyer in the course of storage or handling of the products where that Buyer acts as agent or distributor of the Company's products.
>
> 10.3 The Company shall **not be liable whatsoever** for any **consequential** or **indirect loss suffered by** the Buyer whether this loss arises from **breach of duty** in contract or **tort** or in any other way (including **loss arising from** the Company's **negligence**). **Non-exhaustive illustrations** of consequential or indirect loss would be: loss of profits; loss of contracts; loss of **goodwill**; damage to property of the Buyer or anyone else, and personal injury to the Buyer or anyone else (except so far as such injury is **attributable to** the Company's negligence).

Parties assume that the terms of an **exclusion clause** will be binding if they are contained within a signed written contract. However, legislation **imposes limits on** the use of **unfair contract terms**. One of the two parties may have **greater bargaining power** than the other or may try to bring conditions into the contract whose significance is not realised by the other party. **Disputes arise** around clauses which **purport to**, that is, intend to, limit or exclude obligations **attaching to** parties to the contract. Courts are generally called upon to **construe**, or interpret, the meaning of such clauses.

Note: **damage** – harm done to objects and property; **damages** – money claimed in compensation for harm done
non-exhaustive illustrations – an incomplete list of examples

B Standard clauses

Standard clauses, also known as **boiler-plate clauses**, are generally towards the end of most agreements and frequently include the following:

- A **force majeure** clause, which aims to **release parties from liability for** named risks **outside their reasonable control**. Non-exhaustive examples are: acts of God, fire, flood, earthquake, war, riot, explosion, breakdown of machinery, strikes, and lockouts.

- A **time of the essence** clause, which makes it clear whether or not the time limits contained in a contract are essential conditions.

- An **assignment** clause, which sets out the parties' rights to transfer or **assign contractual rights to** third parties and any need for **prior written consent**.

- A **severance** clause, which provides that the other parts of an agreement continue to **be in force** in the event that some of the **provisions** are held illegal or **unenforceable**.

- A **choice of governing law and jurisdiction** clause, which specifies the jurisdiction and law which will **govern** and **construe** the contract in the event of a dispute.

- A **language** clause, which specifies the language which will **prevail** if the contract is translated.

> BrE: boiler-plate; AmE: boilerplate

Professional English in Use Law

35.1 Replace the underlined words and phrases in the exclusion clause below with alternative words and phrases from A opposite. There is more than one possibility for one of the answers.

> 9.4 Except as provided in Condition 8.3, the Seller will (1) <u>not bear responsibility</u> to the Buyer (2) <u>at all</u> (whether in contract, tort (including (3) <u>carelessness</u>), breach of statutory (4) <u>obligation</u> or otherwise) for any (5) <u>harm</u> or for any direct, indirect or (6) <u>resulting</u> loss (all three of which terms include, but are not limited to, pure economic loss, loss of profits, loss of business, loss of (7) <u>good reputation</u> and like loss) (8) <u>caused by</u> or in connection with:
>
> 9.4.1 any (9) <u>failure</u> of any of the express or implied terms of the Contract by the Seller;

35.2 Complete the standard clauses below. Look at B opposite to help you. Pay attention to the grammatical context.

> 1 The Company shall not be liable for any failure to deliver the Goods arising from circumstances ....

> 2 Time for payment shall be ....

> 3 The contract between the Buyer and the Seller for the sale of Goods shall not be .... or transferred, without the .... of the Seller.

> 4 This Agreement shall be governed by and .... in accordance with the law of England and the parties hereby submit to the exclusive .... of the English courts.

> 5 If any provision of these Conditions is held by any competent authority to be invalid or .... in whole or in part the validity of the other provisions of these Conditions and the remainder of the .... in question shall not be affected thereby.

> 6 This Agreement is drawn up in the English language. If this Agreement is translated into another .... , the English language text shall in any event ....

35.3 Which of the above clauses is

1 a force majeure clause?
2 a severance clause?

Over to you

How does the law regulate exclusion clauses in a jurisdiction you are familiar with? Compare the different types of contract terms in a legal system you know with those set out here.

To look at a recent law report on a contract dispute concerning an exclusion clause, see Price Waterhouse (a firm) v the University of Keele [2004] EWCA Civ 583 at: www.bailii.org/databases.html

36 Privity of contract, discharge, and remedies

A Privity of contract

The principle of **privity of contract** means that a **third party** can neither be **bound by** nor **enforce a term of** a contract to which they are not a party, even though the contract was intended to **confer a benefit on** them. However, since the enactment of the Contract (Rights of Third Parties) Act 1999, such a party may be able to enforce contractual rights depending on the circumstances. If appropriate, it is now usual for contracts to include a clause which **provides** that such rights are not to apply.

There are other ways in which a third party can be affected by the terms of a contract:

- A contract may be made by an **agent on behalf of his principal**. Such a contract may be **enforced by and against** the principal.

- It is usual for a contract to contain an **express provision** relating to **assignment**. The **obligations under contract** cannot be **assigned**, that is, transferred, **without the consent of** a party entitled to the benefit of such obligations.

- In **novation** of contract, a subsequent agreement between the original parties and a third party may have the effect of entirely replacing the original contract.

B Discharge of contract

Parties may be **released from their contractual obligations**, that is, may be **discharged, by performance, by breach, by agreement**, or **by frustration**.

If a contract is **substantially performed**, the terms are entirely carried out and there is no **right to repudiate the contract**, that is, to reject it. If a contract is **partly performed**, a **breach of condition** is **committed**. However, if the innocent party accepts the **partial performance**, a **claim to remuneration** may be raised in a court. If there is **defective performance**, for example a condition is breached, the innocent party may have the right to repudiate the contract and treat it as **terminated** once he or she has **communicated acceptance of the breach** of contract.

A contract may be **discharged by agreement** between the parties in a process known as **accord and satisfaction**. If it becomes impossible to perform, for example due to the non-occurrence of a particular event which forms the basis of the contract, or the death of a party, the contract is **discharged by frustration**.

C Remedies for breach of contract

An award for **damages** – money claimed as **compensation for loss** – is the primary **remedy** for a party who **suffers a breach** of contract. In some circumstances, the courts may **use their discretion** to **compel a defaulting party** to perform his contractual obligations. This is known as a **decree of specific performance**. It may not be appropriate if the obligation is not sufficiently clearly defined, or if **enforcement** would require the continual **supervision of the court** over a long period of time. In other circumstances, the court may **grant an injunction** to **restrain** a party from **breaking the contract**. In certain circumstances, for example **misrepresentation**, parties may **rescind**, that is, cancel, a contract and by **rescission** be restored to the same position they were in before the contract was made.

Note: unliquidated damages – the sum of money is fixed by the court.
liquidated damages – the amount is specified in a clause in the contract.

36.1 Complete the definitions. Look at A opposite to help you.

1 .... – a person who represents another in matters relating to a contract
2 .... – a person who, although not party to a transaction between two others, is in some way affected by it
3 .... – the relationship between parties to a contract which makes the contract enforceable between them
4 .... – a transaction in which a new contract is agreed by all parties to replace an existing contract
5 .... – a clause stating a specific condition in a contract
6 .... – to compel the performance of a condition
7 .... – to give money or advantage to someone
8 .... – contractual duties
9 .... – the legal transfer of duties

36.2 A solicitor has given her assistant some instructions. Replace the underlined words and phrases in her notes with alternative words and phrases from B opposite. Pay attention to the grammatical context.

 Happrew &Co

Jane,
Marie's just typed up some background notes from a short meeting I had with a client. Can you look into the following questions and get back to me?
Thanks,
Anna

JJ agreed to build an extension on Mrs B's house for a fixed sum. He did part of the work but wouldn't come back to finish external walls. She believes he went to work on another site. JJ says he broke his leg. Mrs B needed to move into the house and eventually completed the building herself, using building materials left on the site by JJ. JJ is now suing her to recover the value of work done and the materials used. She says he broke the contract.

1 Can she be <u>set free</u> from her <u>agreement</u>?
2 Can she claim there was <u>a fault in the carrying out</u> of the contract?
3 Has a breach of condition or a breach of warranty <u>taken place</u>?
4 Has the contract been <u>completely fulfilled</u> or only partly?
5 Did she <u>let him know that she agreed to the break in the contract</u>?
6 Can she <u>refuse to carry out her part of</u> the contract?
7 Is the contract <u>ended because it can't possibly be fulfilled</u>?
8 Can JJ claim <u>repayment of financial costs</u> for the materials Mrs B used and for the value of work done?

36.3 Choose the correct word or phrase in brackets to complete the sentences. Look at C opposite to help you.

1 A contract may be (restrained/rescinded/compelled) if the court finds there was misrepresentation of the facts.
2 Courts may use (rescission/misrepresentation/discretion) to grant damages.
3 If a party (suffers/grants/compels) a breach, the courts may award compensation.
4 An injunction was (performed/rescinded/granted) to enforce a term in the contract.
5 The court compelled the party in breach to (rescission/misrepresentation/specific performance).

Over to you

What would be the answers to the questions in 36.2 in a jurisdiction you are familiar with? How are contracts discharged in that jurisdiction?

To look at the Contract (Rights of Third Parties) Act 1999, go to: www.opsi.gov.uk/acts.htm

37 Standard terms in the sale and supply of goods

A Using standard terms

Alice Glenn, a solicitor, has been invited by the local Chamber of Commerce to give a talk to a group of young entrepreneurs on **using standard terms** in **business transactions**.

'It's extremely common for **standard terms and conditions** of business to be used by companies whose trade involves **entering into** numerous similar **transactions**, either as a **supplier** or **purchaser**. The aim is to standardise how commercial transactions are to be effected, so as to **produce uniformity** and increase efficiency, and **reduce the need for** detailed negotiation in each transaction by production of standard **terms favourable to** the company.

The standard terms of any company will always be **subject to legal restrictions**, either statutory or common law. The terms must be regularly reviewed to ensure that they don't **conflict with** new **legal developments** and that they continue to **reflect the aims of** the company.'

B Incorporating terms

'Because it's a basic principle of contract law that new terms cannot be introduced after a binding contract has been made, the proposed **standard terms** must be **incorporated into the offer**. For a seller then, it will be essential to ensure that an offer to buy is **on the seller's terms**, for example on a standard order form which incorporates the seller's standard terms and conditions. The offer from the buyer can then be confidently accepted by the seller without the need for further qualification. However, an apparent '**acceptance**' which is stated to be 'on the following terms' could actually constitute a **counter offer** and lead to an unwelcome **battle of the forms**, when both parties seek to impose their own standard terms.

In order to avoid such situations, sellers generally incorporate standard terms in all their communications, including catalogues, brochures, confirmations of order, and delivery notes. In the event of doubt that standard terms have been effectively incorporated into a contract at the offer/acceptance stage, it may be possible to show that they have been incorporated during the course of dealing between the parties, for example where there has been **regular and consistent trading** between the parties.

The object of standard terms and conditions is often to **limit the liability** of the seller, or to increase it in the case of standard conditions produced by the buyer. Such limitation or **exclusion of liability** is **affected by statutory provisions**. In addition, these may **impose implied terms and conditions** in contracts for the supply of goods and services in such a way which **overrides the provision** of some standard terms and conditions. The Sale of Goods Act 1979, which has been amended by the Sale and Supply of Goods to Consumers Regulations 2002[1], imposes implied terms in contracts for the sale of goods, including **warranties** that the goods sold are 'free from undisclosed charges or **encumbrances** (liability or charge) and that the buyer will **enjoy quiet possession** of the goods.' In other words, if you buy something, you should be able to use it without interference. In most of the relevant statutes, there is a distinction made between **consumer contracts** and those which are between businesses.'

[1]these Regulations implement a Directive of the European Parliament.

37.1 Make word combinations using a word or phrase from each box. Then use appropriate word combinations to complete the sentences below. Look at A opposite to help you.

enter into
produce
reduce
reflect
subject to
terms
use
conflict with

uniformity
legal restrictions
favourable to
standard terms
transactions
the aims of
the need for
legal developments

1 The following provisions set out the entire financial liability of XYZ Ltd
....

2 Customers are invited to purchase goods on an applicable order form or otherwise in writing to .... to make an offer.

3 The Interpretation or Definitions section of the Standard Terms is intended to
.... discussion about the meaning of terms and to avoid ambiguity.

4 It is important that the Standard Terms and Conditions of Sale
.... of your organisation, but they also need to be amended in the light of any changes to the law.

37.2 Complete the notes taken by a member of the audience at Alice Glenn's talk. Look at B opposite to help you.

<u>The Use of Standard Terms</u>

1 Each order or .... of a quotation for goods by the buyer from a company shall be deemed to be an offer by the buyer subject to the conditions.

2 Implied into all contracts for the sale of goods is the following term: that the seller has the right to sell the goods and that they are free from .... or charges.

3 Nothing in the conditions shall be an .... of liability for death or personal injury caused by the company's negligence.

4 Any contract between the company and the customer should have ....
the standard conditions.

5 A transaction will be treated as a .... contract unless it is made in the course of a business, and is an integral part of the business itself.

6 When two parties deal with each other using their own respective terms, and these terms conflict, there may be a 'battle of the forms' with offer and ....
....

Over to you

To look at the Sale and Supply of Goods Act 1994 and the Sale and Supply of Goods to Consumers Regulations 2002, go to: www.opsi.gov.uk/acts.htm

How does this legislation differ from a jurisdiction that you are familiar with?

38 Licensing agreements and computer programs

A Licences and software products

Alice Glenn, a solicitor, is talking to a Dutch trainee about **licensing agreements**, also known as **licence agreements**.

'We work in a number of sectors with **licensors** and **licensees**, establishing **compliance programmes** for **licensing and distribution**, and advising on **licensing revenues**. In the computer software sector, the **authorised licensor grants a licence to** a purchaser of the software products, **under the terms of** the licence. The grant of such a licence is often held, or **deemed, to enter into effect** with the initial installation by the purchaser of the product in their computer, or even upon **breaking the seal** of the packaging enclosing the product. In the US this is known as a **shrink-wrap license**. When this happens, the purchaser is deemed to accept the terms and conditions **enshrined within the licence**. Computer programs are specifically **protected by copyright law** in the UK under the Copyright, Designs and Patents Act 1988 as subsequently amended. The Act provides that 'copying' a programme, or anything else falling within the definition of 'literary works', will be a breach of copyright.

The aim of software licences is to **permit** the licensee to copy the software as is necessary for the successful use of the product, whilst **restricting the unauthorised use** of the software. A software licence for products sold in mass will of necessity be **non-exclusive**, as other licences with the same terms will be granted to other purchasers of that product. In contrast, the purchase by a business of bespoke software, that is, made to order software, usually involves the negotiation of a licence which **allows use by multiple systems**, and therefore copying, although the number of users and their geographical location, as well as the **permitted use**, may well be specified. The Licensor will usually **reserve the right to** enter into similar licences with other purchasers. In such licences, the **liability clause** will often be the subject of much negotiation and the means for **enforcing** it will be of concern to the licensor.'

> BrE: a licence; AmE: a license; BrE and AmE: to license

B Exclusion and limitation clauses

'As with any other contract, the licence will contain **express terms** (see Unit 34). These must, however, be interpreted against a background of statutory regulation. The licensor cannot **contract out of** these, although the standard terms of some software licences may claim, or **profess**, to limit the liability of the **supplier** for **loss or damages** arising from the use of the software. The extent to which such clauses will be successful depends upon the loss in respect of which a claim is made, and whether or not negligence is involved. As you're aware, it's not possible to **exclude liability for** death or injury due to negligence. Software licences differ crucially from other copyright **permissions** in that statutory regulation which has been developed alongside the developing technology has **restricted the extent** to which the permissions may control use. For example, the Copyright (Computer Programmes) Regulations 1992 and the Copyright and Related Rights Regulations 2003 **confer rights upon** licensees which cannot be contractually excluded.'

38.1 Replace the underlined words and phrases in the following clauses from software licensing contracts with alternative words and phrases from A opposite. Pay attention to the grammatical context. There is more than one possibility for two of the answers.

1   The <u>purchaser of the Licence</u> agrees to uphold these copyrights.

2   Caklyn Enterprises, Benbecula, is the <u>owner of the copyright</u> of the program.

3   By <u>opening the Package</u> or installing the product, the Licensee agrees to be bound by all the terms and conditions of this Agreement.

4   Caklyn Enterprises grants a non-<u>sole</u> Software Licence to the Licensee.

5   This licence agreement <u>starts to operate</u> at the time you open the Package and is effective until terminated.

6   The Licensee may terminate this <u>official document permitting use</u> at any time by destroying the Software together with all copies.

7   The computer program provided along with this Licence is licensed, not sold, to you by Caklyn Enterprises for use only <u>according to the conditions</u> of this Licence.

8   If the Software is installed on a common disk and used by <u>many</u> systems, an additional Licence must be <u>given</u> by Caklyn Enterprises for each system.

9   The Software is <u>taken care of by law which controls its use</u>.

10 If any provision of this Licence shall be held by a court of competent jurisdiction to be contrary to law, that provision will be <u>put into effect</u> to the maximum extent permissible.

38.2 Choose the correct word in brackets to complete the sentences. Look at A and B opposite to help you.

1   You agree that you will not cause or (exclude/permit/restrict) the removal of any copyright notices from the licensed software.
2   The licensor (reserves/confers/permits) any rights not expressly granted to the licensee.
3   Statutory regulations prevent you from (permitting/professing/excluding) liability under the contract.
4   The agreement (professed/deemed/conferred) to grant an exclusive licence.
5   Use of the supplied software is (permitted/restricted/reserved) to a single machine.
6   The licensee is (professed/permitted/deemed) to agree to the terms of the licence when they open the software packaging.

Over to you

What regulations govern licensing agreements in a jurisdiction you are familiar with? In what situations do licensees or licensors require the services of a lawyer?

To look at a case arising from a software agreement, go to: St Albans City and District Council v International Computers Ltd [1996] 4 All ER 481 at www.bailii.org/databases.html

39 Commercial leases

A Interest in property

Nina Kahn, a partner in a Bristol law firm's **Real Estate**, or Property, Department, is talking to a foreign client about commercial leases.

'In the UK, it's possible to own either a **freehold** or **leasehold** interest in property. Freehold refers to the estate interest where ownership may be held for an unlimited time without paying rent. A freehold owner, the **freeholder**, may enter into an agreement to lease or let the property, permitting **occupation** for a fixed **term**, or time, by another person or company who then becomes the **tenant**, also known as the **lessee** or **leaseholder**. The freeholder is the **landlord**, or the **lessor**. Some commercial properties, such as shopping centres, may have a complex structure of ownership with a chain of **leases** so that the **occupier**, for example the owner of a small shop in the centre, may **sub-lease** or **underlet** from the tenant and be an **under-tenant**, or even a sub-under-tenant of the freeholder, who is the head landlord.'

B Terms of a commercial lease

'A commercial **tenancy**, the agreement by which a person can occupy a property, may be protected by the **security provisions** of the **statutory regime**. This means that the business tenant in occupation at the end of tenure of the contractual term will have a statutory right to a **renewal of the lease** unless the landlord is able to show that the statutory **grounds exempting the right** apply. An example of such grounds would be the landlord's intention to occupy the property himself or to demolish or substantially redevelop the property. Parties may, of course, agree to opt out of the statutory regime.

Commercial leases are often lengthy, complex documents as they set out the respective obligations of the parties in relation to the property, and these may vary. Such obligations would normally include:

- the amount of rent, the method by which it is to be paid, penalties for late payment, and a **rent review clause** establishing when rent may be increased or decreased;
- provisions for the insurance and maintenance of the property;
- restrictions on dealing with the property, that is, whether the tenant is to be allowed to **transfer interest in** the property to someone else, or to underlet to an under-tenant.

Also included among the obligations would be required conditions, permissions and **covenants** (agreements), and provisions for **yielding up** the lease at the end of the term.

A lease must be for a **term certain**, that is, a fixed period. However, it may include a **break clause** which sets out a **Break Date**, either on a fixed date or on a rolling basis, for example anytime after a fixed date. After this date, the party with the benefit of the break option may **exercise the break** by **serving notice** and may **terminate** the lease early.'

C Obtaining leasehold interest

'Where a new **lease** is to be **granted**, the landlord's solicitors will usually produce a draft lease for approval or amendment by the tenant's solicitor. In circumstances where a tenant is **assigning an existing lease**, that is, transferring his interest in the property, the new tenant will **take the lease** as it is and the landlord's **consent to the assignment** will usually have to be **obtained**. This may be subject to certain conditions, such as the provision of **guarantors** for the performance of the lease – normally the outgoing tenant who signs a **guarantee in favour of** the landlord – or the payment of a rent deposit, depending upon the conditions set out in the lease.'

39.1 Complete the definitions. Look at A opposite to help you. There is more than one possibility for one of the answers.

1 .... – a person who is granted a lease by the freeholder
2 .... – property that is held for an indefinite period
3 ....-.................................. – a person who sub-leases from a tenant

39.2 A solicitor is holding an initial meeting with new clients. Replace the underlined words and phrases with alternative words and phrases from B and C opposite. There is more than one possibility for one of the answers.

1
> We've got some questions we'd like you to help us with. What rights would we have for <u>getting the lease extended</u> on the shop?

2
> It depends on whether the landlord gives <u>reasons excusing</u> your rights. Or whether there's been agreement to contract out of the <u>legislative rules</u> for tenancy security provisions. I'll need to see the lease before I can advise you properly.

3
> As tenants, could we <u>give</u> the property to someone else to rent?

4
> You would need the landlord's <u>agreement</u> and there may be conditions. Unfortunately, I've not been sent a copy of the lease yet.

5
> When can there be a <u>change to the rent</u>?

39.3 Complete this extract from a draft lease. Look at A, B and C opposite to help you. Words with an initial capital letter are assumed to be defined terms of the lease.

TENANT'S BREAK CLAUSE: ROLLING BREAK

1. TENANT'S RIGHT TO BREAK

1.1 For the avoidance of doubt, references in this (1) .... to the Tenant and to the (2) .... are to the persons named as such in this lease and to their respective successors in title.

1.2 In this clause:
(a) (3) .... means the date on which this lease shall (4) .... pursuant to this clause, and
(b) **Break Notice** means a notice served pursuant to clause 1.4.

1.3 The Break Notice shall specify the Break Date but shall not specify as the Break Date a date which is either;
(a) earlier than [SPECIFY EARLIEST BREAK DATE], or
(b) earlier than [six] months after the date on which the Break Notice is deemed to be have been served on the Landlord;

1.4 Subject to clause 1.5 , the (5) .... may terminate this lease at any time by (6) .... on the Landlord.

1.5 A Break Notice shall be of no effect if:
(a) the Tenant has assigned this lease before it serves the Break Notice (whether or not it has made an application to HM Land Registry to register the (7) ....), or

---

Over to you

How is the relationship between landlord and tenant regulated in a jurisdiction you are familiar with? What sort of problems may arise in leasing commercial property? How are they resolved?

40 Buying and selling commercial property

A Commercial conveyancing

Nina Kahn, a solicitor specialising in commercial property, is talking to a foreign client about **conveyancing** – the transfer of the ownership of property.

'The principle of *caveat emptor* applies to the transfer of property in the UK. Contract provisions reinforce this by acknowledging that the **purchaser** has had an opportunity to make full investigation of the **title**, that is, the right of ownership, and to check the property's physical condition and any other factors which might affect the property and its intended use.

Generally, a commercial agent will market a commercial property. The **property particulars**, or details, will specify the terms on which the property, or the **lot** in the case of auctions, is to be sold. The particulars show whether it is to be **sold by auction** – sold to the person who makes the highest offer at an auction – or **sold by private treaty** – the **seller** and **buyer** reach an agreement.'

Note: *caveat emptor* – the buyer is responsible for checking what he buys is in good order

B Sale by auction

'If the sale is to be by auction, a legal pack, prepared by the seller's solicitor, will be available to prospective purchasers. It will contain the special conditions and the auction conditions relating to the sale, as well as copies of appropriate **searches** – documents which prove inspection of records, for example about land use and restrictions on its use, such as Local Authority searches and **environmental searches**. It will also contain **planning permissions**, **warranties**, or guarantees, and other documents relevant to the property and to the transfer of ownership, such as **investigation**, or legal evidence, **of** the seller's **title to the property**.

The prospective purchasers must be satisfied with the seller's title and the other information. If necessary, they may raise further enquiries in advance of the **bidding for** the property. The signing of the **sale memorandum** by the purchaser or their agent at the auction constitutes the **contract to purchase**. Sale, known as **completion**, when payment is made and the **deed of transfer** is **passed** to the purchaser, usually takes place at a **completion date** specified in the special conditions.'

C Sale by private treaty

'In a sale by private treaty, the seller and the purchaser may **negotiate detailed terms**, either directly or via agents. The purchaser will **consider searches** instructed by his solicitor. A **full survey** may be **instructed** and the seller will be asked to **provide replies to pre-contract enquiries**, for example about the property's physical state and the property's boundaries. Commercial property solicitors frequently use published sets of commercial property pre-contract enquiries. When the principal terms have been agreed, they may be set out in a document and **circulated as 'Heads of Terms'**. The seller's solicitor will then produce a **draft contract**, also known as a **sale agreement**, which will reflect the Heads of Terms. Conditions of sale common to most property contracts, governing, for example, **proof of title**, how the **deposit** is dealt with, etc., may be **incorporated into the contract** by reference to published Standard Conditions.

Once the purchaser is satisfied with all the information and the **form of contract**, that is, the terms and conditions, has been **agreed**, the parties may proceed to **exchange contracts**. This constitutes a contractual obligation to **complete the sale** or **purchase** on the terms in the contract, and **penalties** will **arise** in the event of **default**. A **conditional contract**, where completion is to take place within a specified period of something happening, will usually contain a **longstop date** – a final date – at which point the parties may **rescind the contract** – cancel it – if the conditions have not been achieved.'

40.1 Complete the definitions (1–7) then use appropriate words to complete the extract from the auction property particulars below (a–c). Look at A and B opposite to help you.

1 .... – law and procedures relating to the sale and purchase of property
2 .... – property sold at auction
3 .... – the right to hold property
4 .... – offers competing to purchase
5 .... – the contract to purchase document
6 .... – owner of a property who transfers the ownership for money
7 .... – specified time when the payment is to be made and the property deed transferred

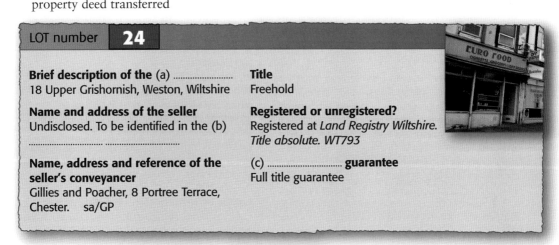

LOT number **24**

Brief description of the (a) ....
18 Upper Grishornish, Weston, Wiltshire

Name and address of the seller
Undisclosed. To be identified in the (b)
....

Name, address and reference of the seller's conveyancer
Gillies and Poacher, 8 Portree Terrace, Chester.   sa/GP

Title
Freehold

Registered or unregistered?
Registered at *Land Registry Wiltshire. Title absolute. WT793*

(c) .... **guarantee**
Full title guarantee

40.2 Choose the correct word or phrase in brackets to complete the sentences. Look at C opposite to help you.

1 The (purchaser/seller/solicitor) considers searches.
2 Parties may (complete/rescind/exchange) the contract in the event that the conditions have not been achieved.
3 A (full survey / pre-contract enquiry / sale agreement) is drafted by the seller's solicitor.
4 The parties (consider/exchange/instruct) contracts once all terms are agreed.
5 Standard Conditions can be (instructed/incorporated/completed) into the contract.
6 The seller is asked to provide replies to (searches / investigation of the title of the property / pre-contract enquiries).
7 Terms are (completed/negotiated/instructed) by seller and purchaser.
8 The (investigation of title / full survey / form of contract) is agreed by both parties.

40.3 Re-order the sentences in 40.2 above to describe chronologically the possible procedures in a sale by private treaty. Use the linking phrases below. Some activities may take place around the same time. The first one has been done for you.

First of all, *terms are negotiated by seller and purchaser* ; then usually
.... and .... After
that, ... and .... ;
then it's necessary that .... and finally
.... However, ...

Over to you

What are the procedures for buying and selling commercial property in a jurisdiction you are familiar with? What sort of problems can arise?

To look at standard pre-contract enquiries for commercial property in the UK, go to: www.bpf.org.uk/.

A Employment law

Happrew & Co | About us | **Services** | Know-how | People | Fees | Contact/find us | Search | FAQs | For our overseas clients

Our Employment Law Department is a specialist team. We advise on relevant law, employment policy and procedure, and the **formation of employment contracts**. We assist in the negotiation and **settlement of disputes**, and take or defend proceedings before an **Employment Tribunal** or in a civil court.

Employment law usually involves a mixture of **contractual provisions** and legislation regulating the relationship between **employer** and **employee**, and governing **labour relations** between employers and **trade unions**, for example with regard to **collective agreements** and **collective bargaining** about conditions of work. Developments in case law and changes to legislation, for example from the implementation of European Community **directives**, affect employers and employees alike. The practice of living and working in different jurisdictions means that lawyers also have to refer to international conventions to establish legal requirements.

The main **statutory rights** of employees include **entitlement to**:

- a national minimum **wage**;
- equal pay for **like work**, that is, broadly similar work;
- a written statement of **employment particulars**;
- an **itemised pay statement**;
- **time off** and holidays;
- statutory **sick pay**;
- a healthy and safe working environment;
- family and parental **leave**;
- protected rights on **transfer of business** to another employer (see the Transfer of Undertakings [Protection of Employment] Regulations 2006);
- **notice of termination of employment**;
- not to have **unlawful deductions** from wages;
- not to be **discriminated against** on grounds of sex, race, sexual orientation, disability, religion, age, **part-time** or **fixed term** employment, or trade union membership.

> BrE: labour; AmE: labor

> BrE: trade union; AmE: labor union

B Contract of employment

It is usual practice for employers and employees to enter into a written agreement which sets out their respective obligations and rights, and which constitutes a **contract of employment**, either at the **commencement** of employment or shortly before. Clauses in the contract generally deal with pay, deductions, hours of work, time off and leave, place of work, absence, confidentiality, restrictions on the actions of an employee once employment is ended (known as a **restrictive covenant**), **giving notice**, the **grievance procedures** in the event of job loss, and **variation of contract** (meaning parties may agree to vary terms of the contract but terms cannot be **unilaterally varied**, that is, by one party without agreement).

Employers are bound by the employment contract and statutory regulation as to how they may deal with employees, particularly in relation to the termination of employment. Failure to observe such obligations and regulations may **give rise to a claim** for **wrongful dismissal** (where the employer is **in breach of contract**), **unfair dismissal** (where the employer has not followed a fair dismissal and disciplinary procedure before terminating the contract), or **constructive dismissal** (where an employee **resigns** because of the conduct of his employer). **Gross misconduct** by the employee, for example theft from the employer, may result in **summary**, that is, immediate, **dismissal**. In other circumstances, the employee may be **made redundant**, for example if the employer has ceased to carry on business.

> BrE: made redundant; AmE: laid off

41.1 Make word combinations from A opposite using words from the box. Then use appropriate word combinations to complete the definitions below.

| employment | bargaining | fixed | tribunal | collective | relations | sick | trade |
| employment | union | particulars | time | labour | pay | off | term |

1 .... – salary paid when an employee cannot work because of illness
2 .... – restricted period of employment set out in contract
3 .... – organisation which represents the workers, who are its members, in discussions of pay and working conditions with their employer
4 .... – specialist court dealing in disputes between employers and employees
5 .... – written details of a position in a company
6 .... – negotiations between an employer and a trade union on terms and conditions of employment and work

41.2 A lawyer is giving advice to a client about an employment contract over the phone. Replace the underlined words and phrases with alternative words and phrases from B opposite. There is more than one possibility for one of the answers.

> I've looked through the contract and it seems satisfactory in relation to (1) <u>the period of warning that the contract is going to end</u>. However, I think you should look for some adjustment on the (2) <u>clause preventing you working in the same field for three years after you've left the company</u>. Other than that, the terms relating to being (3) <u>let go by the company if it fails</u> and (4) <u>being removed from the job</u>, with the related (5) <u>procedure for making a complaint</u> and (6) <u>changes being made to your work</u>, are quite straightforward.

41.3 Which type of dismissal may have occurred in the following situations? Look at B opposite to help you.

1 An employee decides to leave her job because she is moved, without consultation, to a new position in the company which she regards as a reduction in her role. A new post covering broadly the same area as hers is offered to an outside applicant.
2 An employee is forced to leave his job because he has arrived at his place of work under the influence of alcohol on several occasions.
3 An employer has not gone through the appropriate procedures before forcing an employee to leave his job.

41.4 Choose the correct prefix from the box to make the opposite of the adjectives below.

| un | non- | il | ir |

1 relevant   2 legal   3 lawful   4 restrictive   5 fair   6 statutory

Over to you

What are the main statutory and contractual rights in employment in a jurisdiction you are familiar with? What rights do employers and employees have on termination of contract?

To look at more on employment relations and contracts of employment, go to: www.dti.gov.uk/employment/. To see the Employment Act 2002, go to: www.opsi.gov.uk/acts.htm

For details of employment law legislation in the UK, see the Trade Union and Labour Relations Act 1992, the Employment Rights Act 1996, and the Employment Act 2002.

42 Copyright and patent

A Copyright

Trainees at a law firm have been asked to help prepare a section on **Intellectual Property (IP)** law for the monthly e-newsletter circulated to clients. Some of their preparatory notes are below.

<u>Type of IP interest</u>
Copyright

<u>How the interest or right arises</u>
An **automatic right** arising from statute.

Copyright arises as soon as an **original work** (literary, dramatic, musical, or artistic, as defined in the main UK statute: Copyright Designs and Patents Act 1988, and its subsequent amendments) is created and **embodied** in a specific media (for example on film, in a sound recording, in print, or as an electronic record). Copyright also arises in the **typography** (the layout) of the published works.

<u>What protection is available?</u>
It is the **expression** in a particular **tangible form** which is protected rather than the idea itself.

The **copyright owner**, normally the author, has **exclusive rights**, including the rights to make copies, to sell copies to the public, or to give a public performance of the work. The owner may **license**, usually in writing, the **reproduction** of the work.

<u>Action required</u>
The right cannot be registered.

It is possible to use a **copyright symbol** (©) followed by the author's name and date to indicate that it is intended that the work should have **copyright protection**, but it is not necessary to do this.

B Patent

<u>Type of IP interest</u>
Patent

<u>How the interest or right arises</u>
A patent is a **territorial right** given to the **patent holder** for a **statutory period** of years. It must be applied for in each jurisdiction for which protection is required. In the UK, it may be **granted** by the UK Patent Office; in the USA it is issued by the Patent and Trademark Office.

To be **patentable**, an **invention** must:
• be **novel**, that is, not made public anywhere before the **filing date** on which the application/ description is submitted for patent;
• be **capable of industrial application**, that is, use or application in some kind of industry, for example be a process, a material, or a device;
• result from an **inventive step**. In the US, the test is to be **non-obvious**, that is, be something distinctive which could not have been produced by anyone with relatively good knowledge in the relevant area;
• not be an **excluded thing 'as such'** (Patents Act 1977). For example, it cannot be a discovery, a scientific theory, an aesthetic creation or, in the UK, a business method.

<u>What protection is available?</u>
The invention becomes a **property interest vested in** the **inventor**, which he/she can transfer, by **assignment**, to another.

It confers the **right to exclude** others from making, using or selling the invention.
The import into the UK of a product with a UK patent will be **in contravention of the patent**.

<u>Action required</u>
An application should be **filed on the Patent Office** before any steps are taken to make the invention public.

A **patent application** may **fail** or the **grant of a patent** can be **revoked**, that is, removed from the Register in terms of the Patent Acts 1997, if, for example, a successful application is made to the Court in counter-claim on grounds such as:
• the invention is contrary to public policy or morality (for example, human cloning processes) or;
• the person granted the patent does not have **entitlement** to it.

42.1 Make adjectives from the nouns in brackets. Put a stress mark in front of the stressed syllable in each adjective. Look at A and B opposite to help you.

1 Patent holders have (territory) rights over their inventions.
2 Copyright is a statutory right in an (origin) work.
3 A number of rights fall within (intellect) property, including copyright, design, patents, and trademarks.
4 To be patented, an invention must have some sort of (industry) use; this might include, for example, in agriculture.
5 Discoveries of elements of the human body are not (patent).
6 The invention has to be (novelty) and must not have been disclosed before.

42.2 Find four words in A opposite that can be used to make word combinations with 'copyright'. Then use the appropriate words to complete the sentences below.

1 It is essential to identify the first copyright .... before determining whether a particular form of work qualifies for protection.
2 The duration of copyright .... is calculated by reference to the author of the copyright work.
3 Copyright .... in product design and in the presentation of merchandising for products like toys and cosmetics.

42.3 Complete the definitions. Look at A and B opposite to help you.

1 .... – a property right that subsists in certain tangible creative works
2 .... – a right that exists as soon as a work that can be protected by copyright is created in material form
3 .... – the transfer of IP rights from the owner of the rights to another person or organisation
4 .... – having a fixed material existence
5 .... – the right to own a patent
6 .... – the date on which the full description of an invention is formally applied for
7 .... – the criterion for assessing whether an invention is not an obvious development of what has been done before, in the judgement of someone who is skilled in the relevant area
8 .... – not having been disclosed anywhere else in the world before
9 .... – the capacity of an invention to meet the criteria set by statute in order for an application to be granted

42.4 Choose the correct phrase in brackets to complete the sentences. Look at A and B opposite to help you.

1 The Act generally gives the owner of copyright (the right to exclude / exclusive rights / excluding rights) to reproduce the copyrighted work and to perform the work publicly.
2 The patent gives (the right to exclude / excluding rights to / exclusive rights to) others from importing the invention.

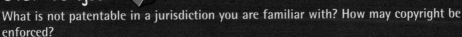

Over to you

What is not patentable in a jurisdiction you are familiar with? How may copyright be enforced?

For information about the Patent Office in the UK, go to: www.patent.gov.uk/; for the US Patent and Trademark Office, go to: www.uspto.gov/web/offices/.

43

Trade marks, domain names, and remedies for IP infringement

A Trade marks and domain names

Trainees at a law firm have been asked to help prepare a section on **Intellectual Property (IP)** law for the monthly e-newsletter circulated to clients. Some of their preparatory notes are below.

Type of IP interest
Trade mark

How the interest/right arises
A trade mark, or **mark**, needs to be **registered** at the Patent Office to be **protected**. A trade mark is **territorial**. It can be a **sign** including words, symbols, or pictures, or a combination of all these elements. Its function is to **represent the goods graphically** and distinguish them from other goods. It is essentially a **badge of origin** enabling customers to recognise a **brand**.

A **service mark** is the same as a trade mark but it **identifies the source** of a service.

What protection is available?
To be **capable of registration**, a trade mark must be **original** and sufficiently **distinctive from** any other marks for the same or similar goods or services. The mark must be specific to the goods or services to which it is to apply and must not be **misleading** or **contrary to law** or **morality**.

In the UK, a trade mark can be **enforced** to protect the mark's **proprietor** under the Trade Marks Act 1994, which implements the EC (European Community) Trade Mark directive.

Action required
Application to the Trade Mark **Registry** at the UK Patent Office for a national trade mark; or for a **CTM (Community Trade Mark)** valid throughout the EU (European Union), to **OHIM** (the Office for Harmonisation in the Internal Market – Trade Marks and Designs); or to the Patent and Trademark Office for **granting of a trademark** in the USA.

Not all trade marks are **registerable**, for example where the shape results from the nature of the goods, such as an umbrella.

The mark may be **licensed** for **authorised use**.

BrE: trade mark; AmE: trademark

Type of IP interest
Domain name

How the interest/right arises
Domain names are unique Internet addresses which distinguish one computer from all others connected to the Internet, for example google.com
Top level domains (TLD) include two letter country codes (ccTLD) such as .uk and .nl. Generic TLDs (gTLD) include .com, .org, .biz, and .coop. Below these are the second level domain names, for example 'McDonalds' in McDonalds.com

What protection is available?
Disputes may **arise** when:
• two or more people are entitled to use the **identical** trademark in different countries and each claim the same domain name; or

• a **third party** registers a domain name the same as, or very similar to, a famous name or trademark, hoping to sell it or to use the business value of a well-known name – a **practice** known as **cybersquatting**, or net name piracy

Action required
Domain names can be registered directly at **accredited registrars**, that is, **Internet name licensing authorities**, or by buying them from Internet naming companies. Names are registered for one or more years, often with annual renewal.

Disputes may be referred to accredited **dispute resolution providers**, such as the World Intellectual Property Organization (**WIPO**), or country registrars.

B Remedies for IP infringement

IP rights can be **enforced** through **civil remedies**, and may involve **criminal sanctions**. As a final remedy, the **rightholder** can obtain **financial compensation for losses** caused by **infringement** by choosing between **damages** or an **account of profits** which the defendant made from the infringement.

Other final remedies may include **delivery up** and **destruction of infringing documents**, a court order to reveal relevant information, or an **injunction**. An **interim** remedy, that is, a provisional one, may include an **interim injunction** to stop an infringing activity, a **search order** to look for evidence of infringement, and a **freezing injunction** to freeze the assets of an **alleged infringer** before trial.

If there is **misrepresentation** as to the **trade origin of goods** leading to damage to the **trading goodwill** of another person, it may give rise to an **action in tort** – a civil wrong known as '**passing off**'.

43.1 Complete the definitions. Look at A and B opposite to help you.

1 .... – anything graphic that conveys information, for example numerals, words, letters, packaging, shape of the goods, etc.

2 .... – using clear images, lines, characters, musical notation, internationally recognised colours, etc.

3 .... – any sign, represented graphically, which is capable of distinguishing the goods or services of one business from others

4 .... – part of an Internet address indicating the type of organisation or country location

5 .... – person or organisation that interferes with or violates another's rights

6 .... – action whereby a person or business registers a domain name and uses it in bad faith or intends to sell it to those who have a legitimate interest in the name

7 .... – a property right associated with the attracting of business custom

8 .... – a civil action where there has been misrepresentation of goods or services leading to damage to the goodwill of a business

9 .... – court order to stop the movement or sale of assets

10 .... – temporary court order until the trial

11 .... – organisations which offer a service to investigate complaints and reach decisions

12 .... – a discretionary remedy available when there has been infringement of intellectual property, involving the award to the rightholder of profits made from the infringement by the defendant

43.2 Replace the underlined words and phrases in this extract from an advertisement for a short course for lawyers on trade marks with alternative words and phrases from A and B opposite.

LawyersForum.com

☐ Register   ☐ Events/Courses   ☐ Jobs   ☐ Updates
☐ Book this event   ☐ Send to a colleague   ☐ Save for later   ☐ Print

Date/time	10 October 2007 10:00 – 17:00
Venue	Manchester
CPD hours	5
Course description	Introduction to trade marks
Course level	Introductory
Delegates	For practitioners with no previous knowledge of this area
Topics covered:	

- Function of trade marks
- Trade marks and (1) <u>product logo</u> recognition
- What is (2) <u>capable of being recorded</u>; ensuring marks are (3) <u>uniquely different</u>; marks that are (4) <u>deceptive</u> or contrary to the law
- How to register a trade mark; application to the Trade Mark (5) <u>office for keeping records</u> in the UK; registering a (6) <u>mark valid everywhere in the EC</u> at the OHIM
- How to oppose the (7) <u>issuing</u> of a trademark by a registry
- How a mark is (8) <u>permitted for use by others</u>
- Litigation, (9) <u>illegal use of a right</u>, and (10) <u>pretence that goods or business are those of another</u>
- Relationship between (11) <u>unique Internet addresses</u> and trade marks
- Internet-based resources

Over to you

What types of trade marks may be registered in a jurisdiction you are familiar with?
What types of dispute can arise over domain names?

For information on registered European Community Trade Marks (CTM), go to: http://oami.eu.int/; for the World Intellectual Property Organisation (WIPO), go to: www.wipo.int/about-ip/en/; for the Internet Corporation for Assigned Names and Numbers (ICANN), go to: www.icann.org/.

44 Information technology law and cybercrime

A Computer security

Pieter den Bieman, a legal practitioner specialising in information technology, is speaking at a Chamber of Commerce lunch.

'I'm sure you'd all agree that the development of information technology and e-commerce has presented exciting business opportunities. However, the increasing sophistication of the systems and applications available to **end users** has created significant **legal challenges** to individuals, companies, the legislature, and legal advisers. The technology necessary to access the Internet has also enabled **innovative illegal activities**. You'll be aware that these include the **breach of computer security** and **unauthorised access to** a computer commonly known as **hacking**. There's also the distribution of **illegally obtained content** from databases, as well as **virus writing** or **virus spreading** achieved by attacks on **insecure servers** which lack adequate protection. In the UK, the **Computer Misuse** Act deals with such illegal use, and also the publication and distribution of material that may be used to aid hacking. Unfortunately, unless you have **adequate security systems** in place, your business is at risk.'

B Cybercrime

'There are **cybercrimes** that may affect you personally, such as credit card fraud online, commonly known as **credit card scams**, and **identity (ID) theft**, when **financial benefit** is **obtained by deception** using stolen personal information. In the USA, **fraudsters**, as they're known, who use a **stolen identity** to commit new crimes, may be charged with what's known in the States as **aggravated ID theft**. The Council of Europe Cybercrime Treaty, also signed by US and Japan, has the aim of international co-operation and **mutual assistance in policing**.

Other cybercrime may impact on your business. There's **cyberfraud**, such as **pharming**, where users are moved to **fake**, non-genuine sites, when they try to link to their **bona fide** bank website. Then there's **phishing**, when a fraudster, by **misrepresentation**, gets Internet users to **disclose personal information** in reply to spam email sent unsolicited to a large number of people. Internet users can also be tricked into **money laundering** activities which aid the transfer of illegal or stolen money.'

Note: misrepresentation – making a wrong statement to trick someone into a contract

C Data protection

'The way you collect, store, and distribute **information that constitutes personal data** on **identifiable individuals** is now subject to **Data Protection legislation**. If, for example, you ask potential customers to supply their address details via the web in the process of requesting further information concerning your business, you should also provide the **data subject** with information about the purpose of collecting the data, the period for which it will be stored, and who will be in receipt of such data. If your web page contains **data relating to specific employees**, remember that this will be **information readily available** internationally and nationally. You must have the consent of the individuals concerned allowing you to make such information available. That **consent must be informed and freely given**. Care must be taken in the management of personal web servers and server software and **clear guidelines given** to staff about your Internet policy in order to avoid **falling foul of the law**, for example the Defamation Act. Finally, in addition to ensuring that you don't **infringe regulations**, you need to consider how to **future-proof contracts** you enter into, by considering potential and unknown developments which may affect your business.'

44.1 Make word combinations from A opposite using words from the box.

adequate	access	misuse	users	computer	breach of
legal	illegally	security	computer security	end	insecure
challenges	activities	virus	spreading	obtained	unauthorised
servers	illegal				

44.2 Are the following statements true or false? Look at A opposite to help you. Use appropriate word combinations from 44.1 to explain your answers.

1 People who use computer applications are known as hackers.
2 It's a legal challenge to gain unauthorised access to a database.
3 Secure servers make virus spreading possible.
4 Distributing illegally obtained data is a breach of computer security.

44.3 Complete the article. Look at B opposite to help you. There is more than one possibility for one of the answers.

Pharming is taking over from phishing

International cyber-crooks have found a new way to rip off the public

Fraudsters find it surprisingly easy to operate credit card (1) .... over the Internet. (2) .... tricks consumers into providing confidential details in response to spam email. Although banks have been raising public awareness of the practice by placing warnings on websites, some customers are still taken in by spam emails inviting them to (3) .... account information.

But phishing is no longer as effective as it was, so (4) .... have developed (5) .... , which does not involve spam email and is harder to detect. The scam redirects users to (6) .... sites when they try to access their (7) .... bank website. A customer logs on, normally using the address stored in his or her 'favourites' folder, to what looks like the bank's internet banking site, but the customer is actually redirected to the fraudster's site.

The fraud is no longer limited to bank accounts. Recent examples have had corporate websites cloned to sell non-existent products, or to get consumers to participate in money (8) .... activities while believing they are dealing with a legitimate organisation.

Whether the fraudsters are using phishing or pharming, criminal prosecution remains difficult, largely because most of the criminals are based outside the territory in which the victim resides. Extradition proceedings are difficult and rare, although some national courts may have limited extra-territorial jurisdiction. Phishing legislation may be drafted but the real problem is the cross-border nature of the fraud. The legislation may have no teeth, leaving the perpetrators almost immune from prosecution.

The Times

44.4 Find more formal expressions in C opposite for:

1 a human person about whom data is stored
2 law which governs the use of computer stored information about individuals
3 willing agreement to something on the basis of relevant knowledge
4 to break the law

Over to you

What problems are there for the law in defining and stopping hacking? What problems are there in balancing freedom of expression and censorship on the Internet?

To look at Internet Law and Policy Forum, go to: www.ilpf.org/. To look at the Council of Europe Cybercrime convention, go to: http://conventions.coe.int/Treaty/en/Treaties/Html/185.htm.
To look at the Computer Misuse Act 1990, go to:
www.opsi.gov.uk/acts/acts1990/Ukpga_19900018_en_1.htm

45 Environmental law

A partner has asked her trainee to draft some notes on environmental law.

A

International environmental law

International environmental law is a fast-developing area affected by scientific discovery and opinion. It encompasses, that is, includes, both international treaties (or conventions) incorporated into national law, and international customary law (general practice accepted as law).
These constitute the law that nation states are obliged to follow or otherwise suffer sanctions from the international legal community. There is also international diplomacy and non-binding instruments which create guiding principles, such as the 1972 Stockholm Declaration and the 1992 Rio Declaration.

The main principles framed in international environmental law are:
- polluter pays principle – the cost of damage is carried by the party responsible
- precautionary principle – to act carefully where knowledge is not certain
- sustainable development principle – to act in the best interest of future generations
- environment impact assessment principle – to use rational planning before carrying out changes to the environment and to consider the costs of ecological effects
- common but differentiated responsibility principle – for countries to have shared but different responsibilities for the environment

B

National environmental law

The critical issues of implementation, monitoring, compliance, and enforcement have to be addressed within legal frameworks. The current impetus to protect the environment at a global as well as a local level means that domestic law in this area has an important interaction with international law. Many jurisdictions have a body of pollution control laws as well as town and country planning law. In the UK, planning law consists of: a regulatory mechanism with a developed process of application for and grant of permission; attaching conditions to development; a system of appeal; rights of public access to information; and rights of public participation.

Planning law has also been used to pursue environmental objectives with the control of development and land through statutory regulations, for example the Wildlife and Countryside Act 1981 and Planning (Listed Buildings and Conservation Areas) Regulations 1990.

Note: listed building – building of special historic interest protected from development and demolition

C

Application of environmental law

Statutory regulation and the role of the various institutions and procedures of legal regulation are frequently complex. The advice of a legal specialist is essential. Due to the potential extent of environmental protection there can be implications for a wide range of transactions and industries. Given that environmental liability can have significant financial implications, such as damages or injunctions, or may even result in criminal prosecutions, lawyers dealing in property transactions or the acquisition of a business will wish to ensure that:
- the due diligence process encompasses a review of any relevant environmental licences;
- relevant audits are instructed;
- and details of any potential, current, or pending enforcement proceedings involving environmental issues are disclosed.

In other circumstances, a client personally affected by pollution or environmental damage may wish to take civil action in tort to remedy the situation.

Note: due diligence – investigation of legal title and company documentation

45.1 Complete the sentences with the principles of environmental law listed in A opposite.

1 If you aim to meet the needs of the present without making it difficult or impossible to meet the needs of the future, this is known as the ....

2 If you make the individual or the organisation that caused the environmental damage cover the cost, this is known as the ....

3 When all countries are expected to make a contribution to environmental protection, but according to their circumstances, this is known as the ....

4 If you act to protect the environment in the case of serious harm, even though clear scientific proof of damage is not yet available, this is known as the ....

5 If you evaluate the suitability and implications of the planned development of land, this is known as the ....

45.2 A lawyer is writing to a colleague about international environmental law. Replace the underlined words and phrases with words from A, B and C opposite. There is more than one possibility for two of the answers.

From:	j.assad@oldfieldslaw.co.uk
To:	c.zurba@oldfieldslaw.co.uk
Subject:	International environmental law

Cassandra,

You said you were interested in getting an overview of international environmental law. You could take a look at *Principles of International Environmental Law*. It's a reasonably comprehensive reference book on regulations relating to environmental (1) <u>defence</u> and the conservation of natural resources. It covers the institutional and legal (2) <u>structure</u>, the (3) <u>written and signed legal agreements between countries</u>, customary law, and all the new case law, as well as issues like (4) <u>agreement to carry out what is ordered</u>, implementation, (5) <u>ensuring that the law is obeyed</u>, and dispute settlement. There's a breadth of topics: conservation of biological diversity, genetically modified organisms, (6) <u>damage through contamination</u> control, hazardous substances and activities, waste management and disposal, the Kyoto Protocol, and techniques for the (7) <u>fulfilment</u> of principles and rules such as environmental impact assessment, liability, and compensation for environmental (8) <u>harm</u>.

45.3 Find words or phrases in A, B and C opposite that can be used to make word combinations with the words or phrases below.

1 review environmental ....
2 instruct ....
3 disclose proceedings involving ....
....
4 suffer ....
5 attach ....

Over to you

What scope is there for legal intervention in environmental problems in a jurisdiction you are familiar with?

For useful links to environmental sites, go to: www.elflaw.org/links.php
For European Environmental Law updates on cases, go to: www.eel.nl/. For the United Nations UNEP conventions and treaties, go to: www.un.org/.

Answer key

1.1
1 Criminal law
2 Public law
3 Procedural law
4 Civil law
5 Substantive law

1.2
1 head of state
2 houses/chambers
3 hierarchy
4 jurisdiction
5 authority
6 conventions

1.3

Verb	Noun	Adjective
'legislate	'legislature	'legislative
pro'ceed	pro'cedure	pro'cedural
con'vene	con'vention	con'ventional
'regulate	regu'lation	'regulatory *or* regu'latory
ac'cede	ac'cession	
e'lect	e'lection	e'lected
'authorise	au'thority *or* authori'sation	'authorised

1 legislature
2 accede
3 procedural

2.1
1 pass/enact
2 enact/pass
3 amend/update
4 repeal
5 codify
6 consolidate

2.2
1 statutory instrument
2 bye-law
3 pressure groups
4 scrutinising the provisions

2.3
1 Bill
2 submitted/introduced/proposed
3 debated
4 enshrines
5 approved
6 re-presented
7 drafting
8 undertaken
9 propose/introduce/submit

3.1
1 bound
2 consider
3 rely on / apply
4 distinguish
5 cite
6 binding precedent
7 revised
8 override

3.2

Verb	Noun	Adjective
a'pply	appli'cation	a'pplicable
pre'cede	'precedent	pre'ceding
per'suade	per'suasion	per'suasive
'bind		'binding

3.3 1 binding 3 citation
  2 applicable 4 persuasive

4.1 1 Magistrates' Court   5 leapfrog
  2 Instance   6 Appeal
  3 Division   7 House
  4 High Court of Justice

4.2

Verb	Noun – event or action	Noun – person
a'ppeal	a'ppeal *also* 'appellate	a'ppellant
'hear	'hearing	
'try	'trial	
'claim	'claim	'claimant

4.3 1c, 2e, 3d, 4a, 5b
  1 Appeal/Appellate
  e appeal
  3 claimant
  4 hear/try
  b tried/heard

5.1 1 warrant of arrest   2 indictment   3 summons

5.2 criminal proceedings; realistic prospect; defence costs; reasonable doubt; guilty plea;
  reduced sentence; severe penalties; indictable offences

  1 realistic prospect   3 indictable offences   5 defence costs
  2 reasonable doubt   4 severe penalties

5.3 1 detained   5 sentence/penalty
  2 acquitted   6 apprehend
  3 appears   7 bail
  4 charge

5.4 f, d, g, a, c, e, b

6.1 1 inspection   5 disclosure
  2 counterclaim   6 witness statement
  3 form of defence   7 practice directions
  4 claim form (formerly known as a 'writ of summons' or a 'summons')

6.2 admit a claim; agree to a stay; allocate to a regime; enforce the judgment; file a reply;
  issue a claim; review the process; serve a claim on; set a timetable; settle differences

  1 Normally the claimant **issues a claim** and it is **served on** the defendant.
  2 The defendant must **file a reply**, whether it is a defence, an admission, or a request for a time
   extension.
  3 Ask the court to **agree to a stay** (in proceedings).
  4 To give parties an opportunity to **review the process** and make decisions.
  5 The claimant can **enforce the judgment** in the Magistrates' Courts.

7.1
1 unfair dismissal
2 defend
3 respondent
4 claimant
5 government agency
6 withdrawn
7 borne by
8 broker a settlement
9 parties
10 witness statements
11 address
12 refer to

8.1 formerly known as; generally called; referred to as; also known as; defined as

1 generally called
2 formerly known as
3 defined as
4 also known as / referred to as

8.2
1 internal
2 frontiers
3 free
4 movement
5 services
6 provisions
7 Treaty
8 States
9 measures
10 obligations
11 Community
12 regulation
13 application
14 entirety
15 applicable
16 directive
17 Member

8.3
1 true
2 false – community rules take precedence. Community law has supremacy over national law.
3 false – the Common Customs Tariff applies to all goods imported into the EU from countries outside the Community like Japan and the USA.
4 true

9.1
1 conveyancing; draw up/draft
2 advocacy; right of audience; appear
3 solicitor; barrister

9.2

Verb	Noun	Noun – person
'train	trai'neeship *or* 'training	trai'nee
ad'vise	ad'vice	ad'viser
'practise	'practice	prac'titioner
'specialise	'specialism	'specialist

9.3
1 degree
2 placement
3 practice/firm/partnership
4 graduated
5 secondment
6 trained
7 specialise
8 corporates

10.1 1c, 2a, 3b, 4e, 5g, 6d, 7f

10.2 1 conversion course
  2 Bar Vocational Course
  3 chambers
  4 pupil master
  5 shadow
  6 document/pleading/(an) opinion
  7 pupillages
  8 tenancy
  9 advocacy
  10 exercise rights of audience ('practise' is also possible)
  11 senior barrister

11.1 best interests; all parties meeting; chargeable work; comprehensive notes; terms agreed; fee earner

  1 best interests
  2 all parties meeting
  3 terms agreed
  4 chargeable work

11.2 a significant proportion of
  a large part of
  a substantial amount of

11.3 1 sound files with the minutes on
  2 copying everyone in / circulating them by email
  3 getting a hard copy of
  4 marks up
  5 type them up
  6 get back to them
  7 get on

12.1 1 District Judge (Magistrates' Court)
  2 Circuit Judge
  3 Lord of Appeal in Ordinary
  4 Lord Justice of Appeal

12.2 1 the Bench 2 the Judiciary 3 the judicial office 4 penal establishment

12.3 1 suspended
  2 imprisonment
  3 applicant
  4 undertaking
  5 injunction
  6 interim injunction

13.1 1 provides/offers
  2 includes/comprises
  3 incorporates/comprises
  4 contains/includes/comprises
  5 led by / headed up (by)

13.2 draw on / have relevant expertise; have exclusive access; have / draw on extensive experience; provide a comprehensive service; make significant investment; resource specialist knowledge

  1 has extensive experience
  2 made significant investment
  3 draw on relevant expertise
  4 resource specialist knowledge
  5 provide a comprehensive service

13.3 1 personnel
  2 submit a tender
  3 professional indemnity cover
  4 transfer know-how
  5 measure outputs

14.1 1 office manual / department manual (or just 'manual')
  2 precedent letters
  3 disbursements
  4 indemnity insurance premium
  5 external auditor

14.2 In a client care letter you should …

    a – … refer to the matter on which you are instructed to act …

    b – … (refer to) the agreed target timescale, such as there is.

    c – … inform the client of who will be undertaking work for them …

    d – … give the name of the person with overall responsibility for conduct of the matter.

    e – … provide a fee estimate for work by staff and should also give the details of any anticipated disbursements, such as court fees, search fees, and other costs. If it isn't possible to give a quote at the outset of a matter you may, for example, suggest that you obtain their approval before undertaking any work in excess of an agreed limit.

    f – … agree to provide an estimate at the earliest opportunity.

14.3 1c, 2d, 3e, 4a, 5b

15.1

1 money laundering	4 as soon as is reasonably practicable
2 one-off transaction	5 exercised all due diligence
3 forestalling	6 disclosures

15.2

1 comply with	6 took all reasonable steps	11 aware
2 Proceeds of	7 exercised all due diligence	12 satisfactory evidence
3 act for another person	8 forestalling	13 nominated
4 contravening	9 disclosure	14 transaction
5 fine	10 suspect	

16.1 1c, 2d, 3f, 4e, 5a, 6b

16.2

    2 Ellipsis – … relating to the above (Project Ivory, Target Company – Franklin Red Limited) …

    3 Substitution of 'this aspect' for 'conditions to which Completion will be subject'

    4 Ellipsis – … read the enclosed (Heads of Terms) carefully …

    5 Substitution of 'the same' for 'the enclosed' Heads of Terms

16.3

    1 true – … enclosed find the further amended Heads of Terms…

    2 true – You will see that I have left this aspect as originally drafted for the time being.

    3 false – As previously discussed, you will let me have further instructions …

    4 false – I should be grateful if you could read the enclosed carefully and confirm that you are happy with the same,

16.4

    1 I am pleased to enclose / Please find enclosed

    2 previously discussed

    3 please let me know if you have any particular concerns / please let me know if we can be of further assistance / if you have any questions, please do not hesitate to give me a call

    4 I should/would be grateful if you could

    5 I look forward to hearing from you (shortly / as soon as possible) / I look forward to our meeting

17.1 You wanted me to give you an outline of the stages in getting proprietary rights. *First*, consider submitting an application to the patent office in the research phase. *Before that happens*, don't publicly disclose the invention because this might be interpreted as prior publication. *Next, / Then, / The next step is to / After that*, think about using the services of a registered patent agent to help prepare the specification (the legal document) required by the patent office. *Once that's been done, / Next, / Then, / The next step is to* complete the form 'Request for grant of patent'. *After that, / Next, / Then, / Once that's been done*, take or send the documents to the patent office. *Finally*, the patent office decides whether the invention fulfils specific conditions before it grants a patent.

17.2
1 equivalent to / the same as
2 differs from
3 referred to as / called / known as
4 comparable to / similar to / like
5 is (very) different from / differs from

17.3
1 in other words
2 that is
3 Let me explain further / Let me put it another way
4 Could I (just) clarify that / So, if I've understood you correctly, / So, if I may (just) check I've got this right,

18.1
1 This Agreement[1] and the benefits and advantages[2] herein[3] contained are personal to each Member[1] and shall[4] not be sold, assigned or transferred[2] by the Member.[1]

2 Lessor[1,5,6] shall[4] not be liable for loss of or damage to any property left, stored, or transported[2] by Hirer[1] or any other person in or upon[2] Vehicle[1] either before or after the return thereof[3] to Lessor[1,5]. Hirer hereby[3] agrees to hold[2] Lessor[1,5] harmless from[2], and indemnify[5] Lessor[1,5] against all claims based on or arising out of[2] such loss or damage unless caused by the negligence of Lessor.[1,5,7]

3 Title[5] to property in the goods shall[4] remain vested in[2] the Company[1,6] (notwithstanding[3] the delivery of the same to the Customer[1,6]) until the price of the Goods[1] comprised in the contract and all other money due from the Customer[1,6] to the Company[1] on any other account has been paid in full.[7]

[1] using capital letters to signal important or defined terms
[2] using legal jargon, including the use of pairs of words or triplets
[3] using old-fashioned words not much in general use
[4] the specific use of the modal verb 'shall' to impose an obligation or duty on someone
[5] using technical terms
[6] avoiding personal pronouns
[7] using long sentences with little punctuation

a Membership
b liable; loss; property; vehicle; arises ('results' is also possible); negligence
c goods; paying

18.2 1f, 2d, 3a, 4g, 5b, 6c, 7e

19.1 1i, 2g, 3h, 4f, 5b, 6a, 7c, 8e, 9d
1 trading vehicle / trading entity
5 general
a duration
c Partnership Agreement
d expelled from
e exemption
f jointly and severally liable
g bankrupt
h sole trader

19.2 Registrar of Companies; minimum authorised capital; security over personal assets; guarantee the obligations; raise share capital; legal entity; Public Limited Company

1 security over personal assets
2 Public Limited Company
3 Registrar of Companies
4 minimum authorised (share) capital
5 to raise share capital

20.1 1 formation agent / registration agent
2 transferred
3 registered company
4 trading name
5 Company Secretary
6 Incorporation

20.2 1 LIMITED   3 registered office   5 mortgage   7 capital
2 ARTICLES   4 objects   6 liability

21.1 1c, 2e, 3a, 4b, 5d
a allot/allocate
b member of the company
c nominal capital
d share certificate
e issuing

21.2 declare a dividend; defer payment; exercise the right; issue at a premium; vote on a resolution
1 vote on; resolution   4 defer payment
2 declare; a dividend   5 issue; at a premium
3 exercise the right

22.1 1 a floating charge   4 security
2 a fixed charge   5 a mortgage
3 a debenture

22.2
1 charge/mortgage
2 mortgage/charge
3 assets
4 debenture
5 creditors
6 insolvent
7 repayment
8 secured
9 fixed charge
10 floating charge
11 defaults
12 charge holder

22.3

Noun – type of legal agreement	Noun – legal person who assigns (transfers) an interest or use in a property to another	Noun – legal person who has been assigned an interest in or use of a property
'charge	char'gor	char'gee
'grant	gran'tor	gran'tee
'lease	le'ssor	le'ssee (*also* 'tenant)

1 chargor   2 mortgagee   3 lessor

23.1
1 He appears to be disqualified. Because he is over 70 a general meeting of the members would need to agree to waive the age requirement. He may also be an undischarged bankrupt in which case the court would need to give leave.
2 The company may be charged a late filing penalty. The directors have committed a criminal offence. This may result in a fine and a criminal record. If this happens again, they may be disqualified from holding the office of director.
3 The Registrar of Companies may strike Monocles Ltd off the register and dissolve the company. The company's assets may become the property of the Crown.

23.2
1e, 2d, 3b, 4a, 5c
a comply with
b provided notice of; statutory form(s)
c served; minutes
d filed/delivered/submitted; within (… months of) the accounting reference date / within the requisite period
e delivered/submitted

24.1
1 creditor
2 insolvent
3 unsecured
4 preferential
5 realise
6 discharge

24.2
1a shareholders or members
1b company directors
1c a creditor or company directors
1d a charge holder or company directors
2 by filing a notice at court
3 by petitioning the court
4 it crystallises / crystallisation
5 it's a going concern
6 winding up or liquidation
7 solvent

24.3
1 on   3 out   5 of   7 in
2 of   4 with   6 as   8 to

25.1

Verb	Noun – concept or object	Noun – person	Adjective
dis'pute	'dispute or dis'pute	dis'putant	
re'solve	reso'lution	re'solver	
con'tract	'contract	con'tractor	con'tractual or con'tracting

25.2

1 parties
2 party
3 resolved
4 dispute
5 referred
6 Contractor
7 Agreement
8 resolution

25.3

1 referral
2 mediation
3 mediator
4 resolving
5 settlement

25.4

1 false – arbitration is a formal and binding process.
2 false – the online mediator passes email responses between parties online.
3 false – adjudication is commonly used to resolve construction disputes.
4 false – the defendant and the claimant are respective parties. The mediator is an independent third party.

26.1

1 notify
2 cooperative
3 stipulated
4 profits
5 due date
6 gains
7 instalments
8 income
9 exceed / be in excess of

26.2

1 chargeable
2 Return (or declaration)
3 due
4 relief
5 exemption
6 bill
7 benefits/efficiency
8 efficiency/benefits

27.1

Verb	Noun	Adjective
com'pete	compe'tition	com'petitive
'regulate	'regulator	regu'latory

27.2

1 regulators
2 takeover
3 (takeover) bid
4 anti trust/competition
5 regulatory
6 merger

27.3

1 abide by
2 offeree
3 relevant securities
4 disclosed
5 offer
6 offeror

28.1

1 a monetary penalty
2 an adverse effect
3 agreed undertakings

28.2

1 inquiry
2 barriers
3 distort
4 harm
5 watchdog (the OFT)
6 refer
7 rivals/competitors
8 investigation
9 referral
10 competition
11 powers under
12 compelled

28.3 1 d – selling popular products below cost price to put pressure on smaller competitors
2 b – erecting barriers to keep out new players; e – acquiring development sites to prevent a rival opening a store
3 b – move into convenience stores could distort competition; d – stores' increasing buying power, which they can use to drive down the prices paid to suppliers

29.1
1 tort	3 damage	5 defamation	7 trespass
2 damages	4 claimant/plaintiff	6 strict liability	8 slander

29.2

Noun	Adjective
defa'mation	de'famatory
'libel	'libellous
lia'bility	'liable
'injury	'injured

29.3
1 injury	6 owes ('has' is also possible)
2 sustained/suffered	7 care
3 undergoing	8 admitted
4 suffered/sustained	9 claim
5 earnings	10 negligence

30.1 1 potential claim
2 adversely
3 impartial opinion
4 a causal link / causation
5 pursue a claim / bring a claim
6 likely
7 on a conditional fee basis / on a no win no fee basis / on a contingency basis (AmE)
8 In the case in point

30.2
1 gives	4 prepares	7 pursue
2 explores	5 keeps	8 affected
3 obtains	6 agrees	9 bring

30.3 Note: The direct object (for example, 'the claim') normally comes before the agent (for example, 'the firm').

2 The claim is explored by the firm.
3 The client's medical records are obtained by the solicitor.
4 A report is prepared by an independent expert.
5 A register of experts is kept by the department.
6 A payment schedule is agreed with the client by the firm.
7 The claim is pursued on a conditional fee basis.
8 The outcome for the patient has been adversely affected by the action of the defendant.
9 The claim must be brought by the claimant within the limitation period.

31.1 1 hire agreement/contract
2 service agreement/contract
3 hire purchase agreement/contract
4 lease
5 loan agreement/contract

31.2 contrary evidence; counter offer; conditions of sale; rebuttal presumption; avoid uncertainty; essential terms; contracting parties; qualified acceptance; subject to contract

31.3 1 An English court is likely to find that no contract was formed. There had been no final unqualified agreement on all the elements of the contract, such as consideration (for example a price) or essential terms (such as delivery). The agreement was vague. There was uncertainty.
2 Helena had become a shareholder. The contract was formed at the time of posting, when acceptance was sent by the offeree, even though the letter in which acceptance was communicated was not actually received. This is the postal acceptance rule.
3 The agreement was legally binding if there was no contrary evidence. There was intention to create legal relations.

32.1 1 authority/capacity
2 (made) in writing
3 have effect / be effective
4 (formally) executed
5 enforceable
6 standard wording

32.2 1 rendered 3 barred 5 set aside 7 required
2 treated 4 consented 6 implied

32.3 1 date of occurrence of the cause of action
2 limitation period
3 lapse of time

33.1 1 Definitions
2 Consideration
3 Recitals (also known as Background or Preamble)
4 Commencement and Date; Parties
5 Interpretation
6 Conditions precedent
7 Operative provisions (referring to those "therein" the Schedules)
8 Operative provisions

33.2 1 Irrespective of / Despite
2 hereby
3 concerning
4 In the absence of
5 vice versa

34.1 1 Where
2 defective/faulty/damaged
3 repair
4 at its sole discretion
5 replace
6 within
7 date of delivery
8 subject to
9 conditions
10 defects
11 due to
12 faulty

34.2 1 breach of contract   3 terminate/discharge the contract
         2 repudiate the contract   4 perform the contract

34.3

Verb	Noun
per'form	per'formance
re'pudiate	repudi'ation
'terminate	termin'ation
dis'charge	'discharge

34.4 'stipulate' does not collocate with 'a contract' or 'the contract'; 'stipulate terms/conditions'
         or 'stipulate a term/condition'

34.5 1 warranty   5 express
         2 damages   6 to the contrary
         3 stipulates   7 previous dealings
         4 implied under statute

35.1 1 be under no liability / not be liable   4 duty   7 goodwill
         2 whatsoever   5 damage   8 arising from
         3 negligence   6 consequential 9 breach

35.2 1 outside their (the Company's) reasonable control   4 construed; jurisdiction
         2 of the essence   5 unenforceable; provision
         3 assigned; prior written consent   6 language; prevail

35.3 1 1   2 5

36.1 1 agent (on behalf of his principal)   6 enforce a term
         2 third party   7 confer a benefit (on someone)
         3 privity of contract   8 obligations under contract
         4 novation   9 assignment of obligations
         5 express provision

36.2 1 released; contractual obligations   5 communicate acceptance of the breach (of contract)
         2 defective performance   6 repudiate
         3 been committed   7 discharged by frustration
         4 substantially performed   8 remuneration

36.3 1 rescinded   3 suffers   5 specific performance
         2 (their) discretion   4 granted

37.1 enter into transactions; produce uniformity; reduce the need for; reflect the aims of; subject to legal restrictions; terms favourable to; use standard terms; conflict with legal developments

1 subject to legal restrictions   3 reduce the need for
2 use standard terms   4 reflect the aims of

37.2   1 acceptance   3 exclusion   5 consumer
         2 encumbrances   4 incorporated   6 counter offer

38.1 Note: It is a convention of written contracts that terms defined within the contract may have an initial capital letter.

1 Licensee   6 Licence Agreement / Licensing Agreement
2 Licensor / authorised Licensor   7 under the terms
3 breaking the seal   8 multiple; granted
4 exclusive   9 protected by copyright law
5 enters into effect   10 enforced

38.2   1 permit   3 excluding   5 restricted
         2 reserves   4 professed   6 deemed

39.1   1 tenant/leaseholder/lessee   2 freehold   3 under-tenant

39.2   1 renewal of the lease   4 consent (to the assignment)
         2 grounds exempting; statutory regime   5 rent review
         3 transfer interest in / assign

39.3   1 clause   5 Tenant
         2 Landlord   6 serving notice
         3 Break Date   7 assignment
         4 terminate

40.1   1 conveyancing   5 sale memorandum
         2 lot   6 seller
         3 title   7 completion date
         4 bidding

         a lot   b sale memorandum   c Title

40.2   1 purchaser   5 incorporated
         2 rescind   6 pre-contract enquiries
         3 sale agreement   7 negotiated
         4 exchange   8 form of contract

40.3 First of all, *terms are negotiated by seller and purchaser*; then usually *the purchaser considers searches* and *the seller is asked to provide replies to pre-contract enquiries*. After that, *a sale agreement is drafted by the seller's solicitor* and *Standard Conditions can be incorporated into the contract*; then it's necessary that *the form of contract is agreed by both parties* and finally *the parties exchange contracts once all terms are agreed*. However, *parties may rescind the contract in the event that the conditions have not been achieved*.

41.1 employment tribunal; collective bargaining; labour relations; employment particulars; time off; sick pay; fixed term; trade union

1 sick pay   4 employment tribunal
2 fixed term   5 employment particulars
3 trade union   6 collective bargaining

41.2 1 giving notice / notice of termination of employment   4 dismissal
2 restrictive covenant   5 grievance procedure
3 made redundant   6 variation of contract

41.3 1 constructive dismissal   2 summary dismissal   3 unfair dismissal

41.4 1 irrelevant   4 non-restrictive
2 illegal   5 unfair
3 unlawful   6 non-statutory

42.1 1 terri'torial   4 in'dustrial
2 o'riginal   5 'patentable
3 inte'llectual   6 'novel

42.2 copyright owner; copyright protection; copyright arises; copyright symbol

1 owner   2 protection   3 arises

42.3 1 copyright   4 tangible form   7 inventive step (AmE: non-obvious)
2 automatic right   5 entitlement   8 novel
3 assignment   6 filing date   9 patentable

42.4 1 exclusive rights   2 the right to exclude

43.1 1 sign   7 trading goodwill
2 graphically   8 passing off
3 trade mark   9 freezing injunction
4 top level domain / TLD   10 interim injunction
5 infringer   11 dispute resolution providers
6 cybersquatting (also known as 'net name piracy')   12 account of profits

43.2
1 brand
2 registerable
3 distinctive
4 misleading
5 Registry
6 Community Trade Mark / CTM
7 granting
8 licensed
9 infringement
10 passing off
11 domain names

44.1 Note: Other common word combinations not shown in text A are in brackets.

breach of computer security (*also* breach of security); illegally obtained; adequate security (*also* adequate computer security); virus spreading; insecure servers; computer misuse; unauthorised access (*also* unauthorised activities *and* unauthorised users); legal challenges; end users (*also* legal/illegal users); illegal activities (*also* illegal access)

44.2
1 false – People who use computer applications are known as end users.
2 false – It's computer misuse / a breach of computer security to gain unauthorised access to a database.
3 false – Insecure servers make virus spreading possible. Secure servers make virus spreading more difficult.
4 true

44.3
1 scams/fraud
2 phishing
3 disclose
4 fraudsters
5 pharming
6 fake
7 bona fide
8 laundering

44.4
1 data subject
2 Data Protection legislation
3 consent must be informed and freely given
4 infringe regulations

45.1
1 sustainable development principle
2 polluter pays principle
3 common but differentiated responsibility principle
4 precautionary principle
5 environment impact assessment principle

45.2
1 protection
2 framework/frameworks
3 treaties/conventions
4 compliance
5 enforcement
6 pollution
7 implementation
8 damage

45.3
1 licences
2 audits
3 environmental issues
4 sanctions
5 conditions

Index

The numbers in the index are Unit numbers, not page numbers.

apprehend /ˌæp.rɪˈhend/ 5
approach /əˈprəʊtʃ/ 17
appropriate measures /əˈprəʊ.pri.ət ˌmeʒ.əz/ 15
appropriated /əˈprəʊ.pri.eɪ.tɪd/ 22
approval /əˈpruː.vᵊl/ 14
approve /əˈpruːv/ 2
approximating /əˈprɒk.sɪ.meɪ.tɪŋ/ 17
arbitration /ˌɑː.bɪˈtreɪ.ʃᵊn/ 25
arbitrator /ˈɑː.bɪ.treɪ.təʳ/ 25
arise /əˈraɪz/ 40, 42, 43
Articles of Incorporation /ˌɑː.tɪ.kl.z əv ɪn.kɔː.pᵊrˈeɪ.ʃᵊn/ 20
as a result of /æz ə rɪˈzʌlt ɒv/ 29
as far as … is concerned /æz ˌfɑːr æz … ɪz kənˈsɜːnd/ 14
as soon as reasonably practicable /æz ˌsuːn æz ˌriː.zᵊn.ə.bli ˈpræk.tɪ.kə.bl/ 15
as well as /æz ˈwel æz/ 14
aspect /ˈæs.pekt/ 15
Assembly (Welsh, Northern Ireland) /əˈsem.bli/ 1
assets /ˈæs.ets/ 22, 23
assign a lease /əˌsaɪn əˈliːs/ 39
assign contractual rights to /əˌsaɪn kənˌtræk.tju.ᵊl ˈraɪts tuː/ 35
assign obligations /ˌəsaɪn ɒb.lɪˈgeɪ.ʃᵊnz/ 36
assignment /əˈsaɪn.mənt/ 36, 42
assignment clause /əˈsaɪn.mənt ˌklɔːz/ 35
association /əˌsəʊ.siˈeɪ.ʃᵊn/ 26
at a discount /æt əˈdɪs.kaʊnt/ 21
at a premium /æt əˈpriː.mi.əm/ 21
at completion /æt kəmˈpliː.ʃᵊn/ 33
at its sole discretion /æt ɪts ˌsəʊl dɪˈskreʃ.ᵊn/ 34
at the earliest opportunity /æt ði ˌɜː.liəst ɒp.əˈtjuː.nə.ti/ 14
at the outset /æt ði ˈaʊt.set/ 14, 30
attach conditions (to development) /əˌtætʃ kənˈdɪʃ.ᵊnz/ 45
attaching to /əˈtæt.ʃɪŋ tuː/ 35
attributable to /əˈtrɪb.ju.tə.bl tuː/ 35
attributed to /əˈtrɪb.ju.tɪd tuː/ 33

auction /ˈɔːk.ʃᵊn/ 31
audit /ˈɔː.dɪt/ 45
authorised licensor /ˌɔː.θər.aɪzd ˈlaɪ.sənts.ɔːr/ 38
authorised by /ˈɔː.θᵊr.aɪzd baɪ/ 1
authorised share capital /ˌɔː.θᵊr.aɪzd ˈʃeə ˌkæp.ɪ.tᵊl/ 20
authorised use /ˌɔː.θᵊr.aɪzd ˈjuːs/ 43
authority to act /ɔːˌθɒr.ɪ.ti tu ˈækt/ 32
automatic right /ˌɔː.tə.mæt.ɪk ˈraɪt/ 42
avoid uncertainty /əˌvɔɪd ʌnˈsɜː.tᵊn.ti/ 31
avoided /əˈvɔɪ.dɪd/ 32
award damages /əˌwɔːd ˈdæm.ɪ.dʒɪz/ 29
Bachelor of Laws (LLB) /ˌbætʃ.ᵊl.ər əv ˈlɔːz/ 10
background /ˈbæk.graʊnd/ 33
badge of origin /ˌbædʒ əv ˈɒr.ɪ.dʒɪn/ 43
bail /beɪl/ 5
balance sheet /ˈbæl.ᵊnts ˌʃiːt/ 21
bankrupt /ˈbæŋ.krʌpt/ 19, 23
Bar Council /ˈbɑː ˌkaʊnt.sᵊl/ 10
bar from /ˈbɑː frɒm/ 32
Bar Vocational Course (BVC) /ˌbɑː vəʊˈkeɪ.ʃᵊn.ᵊl ˌkɔːs/ 10
bargaining power /ˈbɑː.gɪ.nɪŋ ˌpaʊəʳ/ 35
barriers to competition /ˌbær.i.əz tə kɒm.pəˈtɪʃ.ᵊn/ 28
barrister /ˈbær.ɪ.stəʳ/ 9, 10
battle of the forms /ˌbæt.l əv ðə ˈfɔːmz/ 37
become law /bɪˌkʌm ˈlɔː/ 2
(the) bench /bentʃ/ 12
Bench Books /ˈbentʃ ˌbʊks/ 12
bid for /ˈbɪd fɔːʳ/ 40
Bill /bɪl/ 2
binding agreement /ˌbaɪn.dɪŋ əˈgriː.mənt/ 31
binding contract /ˌbaɪn.dɪŋ ˈkɒn.trækt/ 32
binding force /ˌbaɪn.dɪŋ ˈfɔːs/ 8
binding on /ˈbaɪn.dɪŋ ɒn/ 3, 8
binding precedent /ˌbaɪn.dɪŋ ˈpres.ɪ.dᵊnt/ 3
binding upon /ˈbaɪn.dɪŋ əˌpɒn/ 25
boiler-plate clause /ˈbɔɪ.lə.pleɪt ˌklɔːz/ 35
bona fide /ˌbəʊ.nəˈfaɪ.di/ 18, 44

borne by the public purse /ˌbɔːn baɪ ðə ˌpʌb.lɪk ˈpɜːs/ 7
bound by /ˈbaʊnd baɪ/ 36
bound to follow /ˌbaʊnd tə ˈfɒl.əʊ/ 3
brand /brænd/ 43
breach /briːtʃ/ 36
breach of condition /ˌbriːtʃ əv kənˈdɪʃ.ᵊn/ 36
breach of contract /ˌbriːtʃ əv ˈkɒn.trækt/ 6, 34, 35, 36, 41
breach of duty /ˌbriːtʃ əv ˈdjuː.ti/ 35
breach of a duty of care /ˌbriːtʃ əv ə ˌdjuː.ti əv ˈkeəʳ/ 29
breach of computer security /ˌbriːtʃ əv kəmˌpjuː.tə sɪˈkjʊə.rɪ.ti/ 44
breach of warranty /ˌbriːtʃ əv ˈwɒr.ᵊn.ti/ 34
break clause /ˈbreɪk ˌklɔːz/ 39
Break Date /ˈbreɪk ˌdeɪt/ 39
break the contract /ˌbreɪk ðə ˈkɒn.trækt/ 36
break the seal /ˌbreɪk ðə ˈsiːl/ 38
bring a claim /ˌbrɪŋ əˈkleɪm/ 30
bring before /ˈbrɪŋ bɪˌfɔːʳ/ 7
broker a settlement /ˌbrəʊ.kər əˈset.l.mənt/ 7
burden of proof /ˌbɜː.dən əv ˈpruːf/ 5
business organisation /ˌbɪz.nɪs ɔː.gᵊn.a ɪˈzeɪ.ʃᵊn/ 19
business relationship /ˌbɪz.nɪs rɪˈleɪ.ʃᵊn.ʃɪp/ 15
business transaction /ˌbɪz.nɪs trænˈzæk.ʃᵊn/ 37
buyer /ˈbaɪ.əʳ/ 40
by agreement /baɪ əˈgriː.mənt/ 36
by breach /baɪ ˈbriːtʃ/ 36
by common law /baɪ ˌkɒm.ən ˈlɔː/ 34
by custom /baɪ ˈkʌs.təm/ 34
by frustration /baɪ frʌsˈtreɪ.ʃᵊn/ 36
by performance /baɪ pəˈfɔː.mənts/ 36
by statute /baɪ ˈstætʃ.uːt/ 34
bye-laws /ˈbaɪ.lɔːz/ 2
Bylaws /ˈbaɪ.lɔːz/ 20
called to the Bar /ˌkɔːl tə ðə ˈbɑːʳ/ 10
capable of /ˈkeɪ.pə.bl əv/ 31, 42, 43

criminal court /'krɪm.ɪ.nəl ˌkɔːt/ 4

criminal justice /ˌkrɪm.ɪ.nəl 'dʒʌs.tɪs/ 5

criminal law /ˌkrɪm.ɪ.nəl 'lɔː/ 1

criminal offence /ˌkrɪm.ɪ.nəl ə'fents/ 5

criminal proceedings /ˌkrɪm.ɪ.nəl prəʊ'siː.dɪŋz/ 5

criminal sanctions /ˌkrɪm.ɪ.nəl 'sæŋk.ʃᵊnz/ 43

cross-examination /ˌkrɒs.ɪg.zæm.ɪ'neɪ.ʃᵊn/ 5

Crown Court /ˌkraʊn 'kɔːt/ 4, 5

crystallisation /ˌkrɪs.tᵊl.aɪ'zeɪ.ʃᵊn/ 22

crystallise /'krɪs.tᵊl.aɪz/ 22, 24

customary /'kʌs.tə.mᵊr.i/ 34

customary law /ˌkʌs.tə.mᵊr.i 'lɔː/ 45

customs duties /'kʌs.təmz ˌdjuː.tiz/ 8

customs union /'kʌs.təmz ˌjuː.ni.ən/ 8

cybercrime /'saɪ.bəˌkraɪm/ 44

cyberfraud /'saɪ.bəˌfrɔːd/ 44

cybersquatting /'saɪ.bəˌskwɒt.ɪŋ/ 43

damage /'dæm.ɪdʒ/ 29, 35, 45

damaged /'dæm.ɪdʒt/ 34

damages /'dæm.ɪ.dʒɪz/ 29, 30, 34, 35, 36, 38, 43, 45

data protection /ˌdeɪ.tə prə'tek.ʃᵊn/ 44

Data protection legislation /ˌdeɪ.tə prə'tek.ʃᵊn ledʒ.ɪˌsleɪ.ʃᵊn/ 44

data relating to specific employees /ˌdeɪ.tə rɪˌleɪ.tɪŋ tuː spəˌsɪf.ɪk ɪm'plɔɪ.iːz/ 44

data subject /'deɪ.tə ˌsʌb.dʒekt/ 44

date of delivery /ˌdeɪt əv dɪ'lɪv.ᵊr.i/ 34

date of occurrence /ˌdeɪt əv ə'kʌr.ᵊnts/ 32

de facto /ˌdeɪ'fæk.təʊ/ 18

de jure /ˌdeɪ'dʒʊə.reɪ/ 18

deal with /'dɪəl wɪð/ 15

dealing disclosure requirements /ˌdiː.lɪŋ dɪ'skləʊ.ʒᵊ rɪˌkwaɪə.mənts/ 27

debate /dɪ'beɪt/ 2

debenture /dɪ'ben.tʃəʳ/ 22

debt financing /'det ˌfaɪ.nænt.sɪŋ/ 22

debt repayment /'det rɪˌpeɪ.mənt/ 6

debts /dets/ 19

decisions (of higher courts) /dɪ'sɪʒ.ᵊnz/ 7

Decisions (of the European Court of Justice) /dɪ'sɪʒ.ənz/ 8

declare a dividend /dɪˌkleər ə 'dɪv.ɪ.dend/ 21

decree of specific performance /dɪˌkriː əv spəˌsɪf.ɪk pə'fɔː.mənts/ 36

dedicated /'ded.ɪ.keɪ.tɪd/ 13

deed /diːd/ 32

deed is delivered /ˌdiːd ɪz dɪ'lɪv.əd/ 32

deed of transfer /ˌdiːd əv 'træns.fɜːʳ/ 40

deemed to /'diːmd tuː/ 38

defamation /def.ə'meɪ.ʃᵊn/ 29

default /dɪ'fɒlt/ 22, 23, 40

defaulting /dɪ'fɒlt.ɪŋ/ 23

defaulting party /dɪ'fɒl.tɪŋ ˌpɑː.ti/ 36

defect /'diː.fekt/ 29, 32

defective /dɪ'fek.tɪv/ 32, 34

defective performance /dɪˌfek.tɪv pə'fɔː.mənts/ 36

defence costs /dɪ'fents ˌkɒsts/ 5

defend the claim /dɪ'fend ðə ˌkleɪm/ 6, 7

defendant /dɪ'fen.dᵊnt/ 6

deferred payment /dɪˌfɜːd 'peɪ.mənt/ 21

defined as /dɪ'faɪnd æz/ 8

defined terms /dɪˌfaɪnd 'tɜːmz/ 33

definitions /def.ɪ'nɪʃ.ᵊnz/ 33

degree /dɪ'griː/ 9

delegated legislation /ˌdel.ɪ.geɪ.tɪd ledʒ.ɪ'sleɪ.ʃᵊn/ 2

deliver to /dɪ'lɪv.ə tuː/ 23

delivery up (of documents) /dɪˌlɪv.ər.i 'ʌp/ 43

denoting /dɪ'nəʊ.tɪŋ/ 33

department manual /dɪˌpɑːt.mənt 'mæn.ju.əl/ 14

deposit /dɪ'pɒz.ɪt/ 40

Deputy District Judge /ˌdep.jʊ.ti ˌdɪs.trɪkt 'dʒʌdʒ/ 12

despite /dɪ'spaɪt/ 33

destruction of /dɪ'strʌk.ʃᵊn ɒv/ 43

detain suspects /dɪˌteɪn 'sʌspekts/ 5

determine construction /dɪˌtɜː.mɪn kən'strʌk.ʃᵊn/ 33

differ from /'dɪf.ə frɒm/ 17

different from /'dɪf.ᵊr.ᵊnt frɒm/ 17

direct and forcible injury /daɪˌrekt ᵊn ˌfɔː.sɪ.bl 'ɪn.dʒᵊr.i/ 29

direct effect /daɪˌrekt ɪ'fekt/ 8

directive /daɪ'rek.tɪv/ 8, 41

directly applicable in /daɪˌrekt.li ə'plɪk.ə.bl ɪn/ 8

discharge debt /ˌdɪsˌtʃɑːdʒ 'det/ 24

discharge of contract /ˌdɪsˌtʃɑːdʒ əv 'kɒn.trækt/ 36

discharged /dɪs'tʃɑːdʒt/ 34, 36

discharged by agreement /dɪsˌtʃɑːdʒt baɪ ə'griː.mənt/ 36

discharged by frustration /dɪsˌtʃɑːdʒt baɪ frʌs'treɪ.ʃᵊn/ 36

disclose dealings /dɪˌskləʊz 'diː.lɪŋz/ 27

disclose pending enforcement proceedings /dɪˌskləʊz ˌpen.dɪŋ ɪn'fɔː.smənt prəʊˌsiː.dɪŋz/ 45

disclose personal information /dɪˌskləʊz ˌpɜː.sᵊn.ᵊl ɪn.fə'meɪ.ʃᵊn/ 44

disclosure /dɪ'skləʊ.ʒəʳ/ 5, 6, 15

discretion /dɪ'skreʃ.ᵊn/ 36

discriminate against /dɪ'skrɪm.ɪ.neɪt əˌgentst/ 41

disputant /dɪ'spjuː.tənt/ 25

dispute /dɪ'spjuːt/ 7, 33, 43

dispute resolution clause /dɪˌspjuːt rez.ə'luː.ʃᵊn ˌklɔːz/ 25

dispute resolution provider /dɪˌspjuːt rez.ə'luː.ʃᵊn prəˌvaɪ.dəʳ/ 43

dispute resolver /dɪˌspjuːt rɪ'zɒlvəʳ/ 25

disputes arise /dɪˌspjuːts ə'raɪz/ 35, 43

disqualification from /dɪ.skwɒl.ɪ.fɪ'keɪ.ʃᵊn frɒm/ 23

disqualified /dɪ'skwɒl.ɪ.faɪd/ 23

dissolve /dɪ'zɒlv/ 23

distinctive from /dɪ'stɪŋk.tɪv frɒm/ 43

distinguish the case (from) /dɪ'stɪŋ.gwɪʃ ðə ˌkeɪs/ 3

distort competition /dɪˌstɔːt kɒm.pə'tɪʃ.ᵊn/ 28

District Judge /ˌdɪs.trɪkt 'dʒʌdʒ/ 12

exercise the right /ˌek.sə.saɪz ðə ˈraɪt/ 21

expel from /ɪkˈspel frɒm/ 19

expert /ˈek.spɜːt/ 30

expertise /ˌek.spɜːˈtiːz/ 7, 13

explain further /ɪkˌspleɪn ˈfɜː.ðəʳ/ 17

explain procedures /ɪkˌspleɪn prəˈsiː.dʒəz/ 17

explore the claim /ɪkˌsplɔː ðə ˈkleɪm/ 30

express provision /ɪkˌspres prəˈvɪʒ.ᵊn/ 36

express terms /ɪkˌspres ˈtɜːmz/ 34, 38

expression /ɪkˈspreʃ.ᵊn/ 42

expressly /ɪkˈspres.li/ 34

extensive experience /ɪkˌsten.sɪv ɪkˈspɪə.ri.ᵊnts/ 13

external auditor /ɪkˌstɜː.nəl ˈɔː.dɪt.əʳ/ 14

face value /ˈfeɪs ˌvæl.juː/ 21

facility letter /fəˈsɪl.ɪ.ti ˌlet.əʳ/ 22

fail /feɪl/ 42

fail to appear (for trial) /ˌfeɪl tu əˈpɪəʳ/ 5

fake /feɪk/ 44

fall foul of the law /ˌfɔːl ˌfaʊl əv ðə ˈlɔː/ 44

fast track /ˈfɑːst ˌtræk/ 6

faulty /ˈfɒl.ti/ 34

favourable to /ˈfeɪ.vᵊr.ə.bl tuː/ 37

fee earner /ˈfiː ˌɜː.nəʳ/ 11

fee estimate /ˈfiː ˌes.tɪ.mət/ 14, 30

file a reply /ˌfaɪl ə rɪˈplaɪ/ 6

file a return /ˌfaɪl ə rɪˈtɜːn/ 23

file documents /ˌfaɪl ˈdɒk.ju.mənts/ 23

file notice at court /ˌfaɪl ˌnəʊ.tɪs ət ˈkɔːt/ 24

file an application on the Patent Office /ˌfaɪl ən aep.lɪˈkeɪ.ʃᵊn ɒn ðə ˈpeɪ.tᵊnt ˌɒf.ɪs/ 42

filing date /ˈfaɪ.lɪŋ ˌdeɪt/ 42

final claim /ˌfaɪ.nᵊl ˈkleɪm/ 29

finally /ˈfaɪ.nə.li/ 17

financial benefit /faɪˌnæn.tʃᵊl ˈben.ɪ.fɪt/ 44

financial compensation for /faɪˌnæn.tʃᵊl ˌkɒm.penˈseɪ.ʃᵊn fɔːʳ/ 43

financial loss /faɪˈnæn.tʃᵊl ˌlɒs/ 29

fine /faɪn/ 4, 12, 15

firm /fɜːm/ 9

first draft /ˌfɜːst ˈdrɑːft/ 14

first instance /ˈfɜːst ˌɪn.stənts/ 4

fixed charge /ˌfɪkst ˈtʃɑːdʒ/ 22

fixed term /ˌfɪkst ˈtɜːm/ 41

floating charge /ˈfləʊ.tɪŋ ˌtʃɑːdʒ/ 22

for the time being /fɔː ðə ˌtaɪm ˈbiː.ɪŋ/ 16

force majeure clause /ˌfɔːs mæˈʒɜː ˌklɔːz/ 35

forensic accountancy /fəˌren.zɪk əˈkaʊn.tᵊnt.si/ 10

forestall /fɔːˈstɔːl/ 15

form a business relationship /ˌfɔːm ə ˈbɪz.nɪs rɪˌleɪ.ʃᵊn.ʃɪp/ 15

form a contract /ˌfɔːm ə ˈkɒn.trækt/ 31

form a partnership /ˌfɔːm ə ˈpɑːt.nə.ʃɪp/ 9

form of admission /ˌfɔːm əv ədˈmɪʃ.ᵊn/ 6

form of contract /ˌfɔːm əv ˈkɒn.trækt/ 40

form of defence /ˌfɔːm əv dɪˈfents/ 6

form required by the law /ˌfɔːm rɪˌkwaɪəd baɪ ðə ˈlɔː/ 32

formal execution requirements /ˌfɔː.məl ˌek.sɪˈkjuː.ʃᵊn rɪˌkwaɪə.mənts/ 32

formation agent /fɔːˈmeɪ.ʃᵊn ˌeɪ.dʒᵊnt/ 20

formation of /fɔːˈmeɪ.ʃᵊn ɒv/ 41

formation of a company /fɔːˌmeɪ.ʃᵊn əv ə ˈkʌm.pə.ni/ 20

formation of a contract /fɔːˌmeɪ.ʃᵊn əv ə ˈkɒn.trækt/ 31, 32, 41

formerly known as /ˈfɔː.mə.li ˌnəʊn æz/ 8

fraudster /ˈfrɔːd.stəʳ/ 44

free movement of goods, services and capital /ˌfriː ˌmuː.v.mənt əv ˌgʊdz ˌsɜː.vɪ.sɪz ᵊn ˈkap.ɪ.tᵊl/ 8

free trade area /ˌfriː ˈtreɪd ˌeə.ri.ə/ 8

freehold /ˈfriː.həʊld/ 22, 39

freeholder /ˈfriː.həʊl.dəʳ/ 39

freezing injunction /ˈfriː.zɪŋ ɪn.dʒʌŋk.ʃᵊn/ 43

frontiers /ˈfrʌn.tɪəz/ 8

full survey /ˌfʊl ˈsɜː.veɪ/ 40

fully binding /ˌfʊl.i ˈbaɪn.dɪŋ/ 32

fundamental to /ˌfʌn.də.men.tᵊl tuː/ 13

further assistance /ˈfɜː.ðər əˈsɪs.tᵊnts/ 16

future-proof a contract /ˌfjuː.tʃə.pruːf ə ˈkɒn.trækt/ 44

gains /geɪnz/ 26

general application /ˌdʒen.ᵊr.ᵊl æp.lɪˈkeɪ.ʃᵊn/ 8

general damages /ˌdʒen.ᵊr.ᵊl ˈdæm.ɪ.dʒɪz/ 29

general partner /ˌdʒen.ᵊr.ᵊl ˈpɑːt.nər/ 19

general principles /ˌdʒen.ᵊr.ᵊl ˈprɪnt.sɪ.plz/ 8

generally called /ˈdʒen.ᵊr.ᵊl.i ˌkɔːld/ 8

get a time extension /ˌget ə ˈtaɪm ɪkˌsten.tʃᵊn/ 6

get back to (s.o) /ˌget ˈbæk tuː/ 11

get on with (s.t) /ˌget ˈɒn wɪð/ 11

get out /ˌget ˈaʊt/ 11

give details /ˌgɪv ˈdiː.teɪlz/ 14

give judgment in favour of /ˌgɪv ˌdʒʌdʒ.mənt ɪn ˈfeɪ.vər ɒv/ 6

give notice /ˌgɪv ˈnəʊ.tɪs/ 41

give opinions /ˌgɪv əˈpɪn.jənz/ 10

give rise to /ˌgɪv ˈraɪz tuː/ 1, 34, 41

go on appeal from /ˌgəʊ ɒn əˈpiːl frɒm/ 4

go on appeal to /ˌgəʊ ɒn əˈpiːl tuː/ 4

going concern /ˌgəʊ.ɪŋ kənˈsɜːn/ 24

goods /gʊdz/ 43

goodwill /gʊdˈwɪl/ 35

govern /ˈgʌv.ᵊn/ 35

government agency /ˌgʌv.ᵊn.mənt ˈeɪ.dʒᵊnt.si/ 7

government Bill /ˌgʌv.ᵊn.mənt ˈbɪl/ 2

graduated /ˈgræd.ju.eɪ.tɪd/ 9

grant a debenture /ˌgrɑːnt ə ˈdeb.ən.tʃəʳ/ 22

grant a lease /ˌgrɑːnt ə ˈliːs/ 39

grant a licence /ˌgrɑːnt ə ˈlaɪ.sᵊnts/ 38

grant a patent /ˌgrɑːnt ə ˈpeɪ.tᵊnt/ 42

grant a trademark /ˌgrɑːnt ə ˈtreɪd.mɑːk/ 43

grant an injunction /ˌgrɑːnt ən ɪnˈdʒʌŋk.ʃᵊn/ 12, 36

grant bail /ˌgrɑːnt ˈbeɪl/ 5

grant leave to appeal /ˌgrɑːnt ˌliːv tu əˈpiːl/ 4

grievance procedures
/ˈgriː.vᵊnts prə,siː.dʒəz/ 41

gross misconduct /ˌgrəʊs
mɪsˈkɒn.dʌkt/ 41

grounds /graʊndz/ 19

grounds exempting the right
/ˌgraʊndz ɪg,zemp.tɪŋ ðə
ˈraɪt/ 39

grounds for believing
/ˌgraʊndz fɔː bɪˈliː.vɪŋ/ 5

guarantee in favour of
/ˌgær.ᵊn.tiː ɪn ˈfeɪ.vəʳ ɒv/ 39

guarantee the obligations
/ˌgær.ᵊn.tiː ðiː
ɒb.lɪˈgeɪ.ʃᵊnz/ 19

guarantor /ˌgær.ᵊnˈtɔːʳ/ 39

guidelines /ˈgaɪd.laɪnz/ 44

guiding principle /ˌgaɪ.dɪŋ
ˈprɪnt.sɪ.pl/ 27, 45

hacking /ˈhæ.kɪŋ/ 44

hard copy /ˌhɑː.d ˈkɒp.i/
11, 14

harm /hɑːm/ 4, 28, 29

have effect /ˌhæv ɪˈfekt/ 32

head of state /ˌhed əv ˈsteɪt/ 1

head up /ˌhed ˈʌp/ 11, 13

heading /ˈhed.ɪŋ/ 33

Heads of Terms /ˌhedz əv
ˈtɜːmz/ 16, 40

hear evidence /ˌhɪər ˈev.ɪ.dᵊnts/
4

hearing /ˈhɪə.rɪŋ/ 28

hearing of the application
/ˌhɪə.rɪŋ əv ðiː æp.lɪˈkeɪ.ʃᵊn/
12

hereafter /ˌhɪəˈrɑːf.təʳ/ 18

hereby /ˌhɪəˈbaɪ/ 18, 33

herein /ˌhɪəˈrɪn/ 18

hereof /ˌhɪəˈrɒv/ 18

hereto /ˌhɪəˈtuː/ 18

herewith /ˌhɪəˈwɪð/ 18

hesitate /ˈhez.ɪ.teɪt/ 16

hierarchical /ˌhaɪəˈrɑː.kɪ.kᵊl/
12

hierarchy of the courts
/ˌhaɪə.rɑː.ki əv ðə ˈkɔːts/ 1,
3, 12

High Court Judge /ˌhaɪ ˌkɔːt
ˈdʒʌdʒ/ 12

High Court of Justice /ˌhaɪ
ˌkɔːt əv ˈdʒʌs.tɪs/ 4

high quality /ˌhaɪ ˈkwɒl.ɪ.ti/ 13

hire contract /ˈhaɪə
ˌkɒn.trækt/ 31

hire purchase agreement /ˌhaɪə
ˈpɜː.tʃəs ə,griː.mənt/ 31

hold the office of /ˌhəʊld ðiː
ˈɒf.ɪs ɒv/ 23

hold the office of director
/ˌhəʊld ðiː ˌɒf.ɪs ɒv
da ɪˈrek.təʳ/ 23

hostile takeover /ˈhɒs.taɪl
ˌteɪk.əʊ.vəʳ/ 27

House of Lords /ˌhaʊs əv
ˈlɔːdz/ 4

housing association /ˈhaʊ.zɪŋ
ə.səʊ.si,eɪ.ʃᵊn/ 26

human rights /ˌhjuː.mən
ˈraɪts/ 8

identical /aɪˈden.tɪ.kᵊl/ 43

identifiable individuals
/aɪ,den.tɪ.faɪ.ə.bl
ɪn.dɪˈvɪd.ju.əlz/ 44

identification procedures
/aɪ,den.tɪ.fɪˈkeɪ.ʃᵊn
prə,siː.dʒəz/ 14, 15

identified /aɪˈden.tɪ.faɪd/ 15

identify the source
/aɪ,den.tɪ.faɪ ðə ˈsɔːs/ 43

identity /aɪˈden.tɪ.ti/ 15

identity theft /aɪˈden.tɪ.ti ˌθeft/
44

i.e. (id est /ɪd est/) 18

illegally obtained content
/ɪ,liː.gᵊl.i əb,teɪnd ˈkɒn.tent/
44

impartial opinion /ɪm,pɑː.ʃᵊl
əˈpɪn.jən/ 30

implementation
/ˌɪm.plɪ.menˈteɪ.ʃᵊn/ 45

implied conditions /ɪm,plaɪd
kənˈdɪʃ.ᵊnz/ 34

implied from conduct /
ɪm,plaɪd frəm ˈkɒn.dʌkt/ 32

implied into the contract /
ɪm,plaɪd ɪn.tuː ðə
ˈkɒn.trækt/ 34

implied terms /ɪm,plaɪd ˈtɜːmz/
34, 37

implied under statute /ɪm,plaɪd
ʌn.də ˈstæt ʃ.uːt/ 34

impose a duty on /ɪm,pəʊz ə
ˈdjuː.ti ɒn/ 8

impose a monetary penalty
/ɪm,pəʊz ə ,mʌn.ɪ.tri
ˈpen.ᵊl.ti/ 28

impose implied terms and
conditions /ɪm,pəʊz ɪm,plaɪd
tɜːmz ᵊn kənˈdɪʃ.ᵊnz/ 37

impose limits on /ɪm,pəʊz
ˈlɪm.ɪts ɒn/ 35

imprisonment
/ɪmˈprɪz.ᵊn.mənt/ 4

in administration /ɪn
əd,mɪn.ɪˈstreɪ.ʃᵊn/ 24

in breach of contract /ɪn ,briːtʃ
əv ˈkɒn.trækt/ 41

in camera /ɪn ˈkæm.rə/ 18

in contravention of /ɪn
,kɒn.trəˈven.tʃᵊn ɒv/ 42

in curia /ɪn ˈkjʊə.ri.ə/ 18

in custody /ɪn ˈkʌs.tə.di/ 5

in excess of /ɪn ekˈses ɒv/ 14,
26

in force /ɪn ˈfɔːs/ 35

in-house counsel /ˌɪn.haʊs
ˈkaʊnt.sᵊl/ 10

in practice /ɪn ˈpræk.tɪs/ 10

in receivership /ɪn rɪˈsiː.və.ʃɪp/
24

in relation to /ɪn rɪˈleɪ.ʃᵊn tuː/
16, 24

in respect of /ɪn rɪˈspekt ɒv/
38

in situ /ɪnˈsɪt.juː/ 18

in the absence of /ɪn ðiː
ˈæb.sᵊnts ɒv/ 33

in the event that /ɪn ðiː ɪˈvent
ðæt/ 14

in the meantime /ɪn ðə
ˈmiːn.taɪm/ 14

in their entirety /ɪn ðeəʳ
ɪnˈtaɪə.rɪ.ti/ 8

in writing /ɪn ˈraɪ.tɪŋ/ 32

include /ɪnˈkluːd/ 13

income /ˈɪn.kʌm/ 26

incorporate into /ɪnˈkɔː.pᵊr.eɪt
,ɪn.tuː/ 1, 37, 40

incorporate terms
/ɪn,kɔː.pᵊr.eɪt ˈtɜːmz/ 31,
37

incorporated into
/ɪnˈkɔː.pᵊr.eɪ.tɪd ,ɪn.tuː/
1, 37, 40

incorporates /ɪnˈkɔː.pᵊr.eɪtz/
13

incorporation
/ɪn,kɔː.pᵊrˈeɪ.ʃᵊn/ 20

incur costs /ɪn,kɜː ˈkɒsts/ 14

indemnity insurance premium
/ɪnˈdem.nə.ti ɪn,ʃɔː.rənts
,priː.mi.əm/ 14

independent expert
/ˌɪn.dɪ.pen.dᵊnt ˈek.spɜːt/ 30

indictable offence
/ɪn,daɪ.tə.bl əˈfents/ 4, 5

indictment /ɪnˈdaɪt.mənt/ 5

indirect loss /ɪn.daɪˈrekt ˌlɒs/
35

induction course /ɪnˈdʌk.ʃᵊn
,kɔːs/ 12

industrial application
/ɪn,dʌs.tri.əl æp.lɪˈkeɪ.ʃᵊn/
42

information readily available
/ɪn.fə,meɪ.ʃᵊn ,red.ɪ.li
əˈveɪ.lə.bl/ 44

information technology
/ɪn.fə,meɪ.ʃᵊn
tekˈnɒl.ə.dʒi/ 44

information that constitutes
personal data /ɪn.fə,meɪ.ʃᵊn
ðət ,kɒn.stɪ.tjuːts
,pɜː.sᵊn.ᵊl ˈdeɪ.tə/ 44

Lexcel compliant /ˌleksel kəmˈplaɪ.ənt/ 14
liability /ˌlaɪ.əˈbɪl.ɪ.ti/ 1, 20, 21, 26, 29, 35
liability clause /laɪ.əˈbɪl.ɪ.ti ˌklɔːz/ 38
libel /ˈlaɪ.bəl/ 29
licence /ˈlaɪ.sənts/ 38
licence agreement /ˈlaɪ.sənts əˌgriː.mənt/ 38
license /ˈlaɪ.sənts/ 38, 42
licensed /ˈlaɪ.səntst/ 43
licensee /ˌlaɪ.sənˈtˈsiː/ 38
licensing agreement /ˈlaɪ.səntsɪŋ əˌgriː.mənt/ 38
licensing and distribution /ˌlaɪ.səntsɪŋ ən ˌdɪs.trɪˈbjuː.ʃən/ 38
licensing revenues /ˈlaɪ.sənt.sɪŋ ˌrev.ən.juːz/ 38
licensor /ˌlaɪ.səntsˈɔːr/ 38
like work /ˈlaɪk ˌwɜːk/ 41
likely amount /ˈlaɪ.kli əˌmaʊnt/ 30
limit liability /ˈlɪm.ɪt laɪ.əˈbɪl.ɪ.ti/ 35, 37
limitation clause /lɪm.ɪˈteɪ.ʃən ˌklɔːz/ 33, 35, 38
limitation period /lɪm.ɪˈteɪ.ʃən ˌpɪə.ri.əd/ 30, 32
limited company /ˌlɪm.ɪ.tɪd ˈkʌm.pə.ni/ 19, 20
Limited Liability Partnership (LLP) /ˌlɪm.ɪ.tɪd laɪ.əˌbɪl.ɪ.ti ˈpaːt.nə.ʃɪp/ 19
limited partner /ˌlɪm.ɪ.tɪd ˈpaːt.nər/ 19
liquidated /ˈlɪk.wɪ.deɪ.tɪd/ 6
liquidated damages /ˌlɪk.wɪ.deɪ.tɪd ˈdæm.ɪ.dʒɪz/ 36
liquidation /ˌlɪk.wɪˈdeɪ.ʃən/ 20, 24
liquidator /ˈlɪk.wɪ.deɪ.tə/ 24
listed building /ˌlɪs.tɪd ˈbɪl.dɪŋ/ 45
litigation department /lɪt.ɪˈgeɪ.ʃən dɪˌpaːt.mənt/ 30
loan agreement /ˈləʊn əˌgriː.mənt/ 31
lodge a claim /ˌlɒdʒ ə ˈkleɪm/ 7
longstop date /ˈlɒŋstɒp ˌdeɪt/ 40
Lord Chancellor /ˌlɔːd ˈtʃaːnt.sˈl.ər/ 12
Lord Justices of Appeal /ˌlɔːd ˌdʒʌs.tɪ.sɪz əv əˈpiːl/ 12
Lords of Appeal in Ordinary /ˌlɔːdz əv əˌpiːl ɪn ˈɔː.dɪ.nə.ri/ 12

loss /lɒs/ 29, 34, 38
loss arising from /ˈlɒs əˌraɪ.zɪŋ frɒm/ 35, 38
loss of earnings /ˌlɒs əv ˈɜː.nɪŋz/ 29
losses /ˈlɒsɪz/ 43
lot /lɒt/ 40
Magistrates' Court /ˈmædʒ.ɪ.streɪts ˌkɔːt/ 4
maintain /meɪnˈteɪn/ 15
make a call for /ˌmeɪk ə ˈkɔːl fɔːr/ 21
make an agreement /ˌmeɪk ən əˈgriː.mənt/ 31
make an invitation to treat /ˌmeɪk ən ɪn.vɪˌteɪ.ʃən tə ˈtriːt/ 31
make an order /ˌmeɪk ən ˈɔː.dər/ 6
make aware of /ˌmeɪk əˈweər ɒv/ 15
make express /ˌmeɪk ɪkˈspres/ 15
make interim payments /ˌmeɪk ˌɪn.tˈr.ɪm ˈpeɪ.mənts/ 29
make redundant /ˌmeɪk rɪˈdʌn.dˈnt/ 41
make significant investment in /ˌmeɪk sɪgˌnɪf.ɪ.kənt ɪnˈvest.mənt ɪn/ 13
mandatory requirements /ˌmæn.də.tri rɪˈkwaɪə.mənts/ 12
mark /maːk/ 43
mark up /ˌmaːk ˈʌp/ 11
market investigation /ˌmaː.kɪt ɪn.ves.tɪˈgeɪ.ʃən/ 28
market investigation reference /ˌmaː.kɪt ɪn.ves.tɪˈgeɪ.ʃən ˌref.ˈr.ənts/ 28
market value /ˌmaː.kɪt ˈvæl.juː/ 21
Master's Degree (LLM) /ˈmaː.stəz dɪˌgriː/ 9
matter /ˈmæt.ər/ 14
matters of fact /ˌmæt.əz əv ˈfækt/ 4
measure outputs /ˌmeʒ.ər ˈaʊt.pʊts/ 13
Med-Arb /ˈme.daːb/ 25
mediated settlement /ˌmiː.di.eɪ.tɪd ˈset.l.mənt/ 25
mediation /ˌmiː.diˈeɪ.ʃən/ 25
mediation organisation /miː.diˈeɪ.ʃən ɔː.gˈn.aɪˌzeɪ.ʃən/ 25
mediator /ˈmiː.di.eɪ.tər/ 25
medical records /ˈmed.ɪ.kˈl ˌrek.ɔːdz/ 30
medical treatment /ˈmed.ɪ.kˈl ˌtriːt.mənt/ 29, 30

meet /miːt/ 13
member of a company /ˌmem.bər əv ə ˈkʌm.pə.ni/ 21
Member States /ˈmem.bər ˌsteɪts/ 8
members /ˈmem.bəz/ 19, 24
members' club /ˈmem.bəz ˌklʌb/ 26
Members of Parliament /ˌmem.bəz əv ˈpaː.lɪ.mənt/ 1
Members' voluntary liquidation /ˌmem.bəz ˌvɒl.ən.tri lɪk.wɪˈdeɪ.ʃən/ 24
Memorandum and Articles of Association /mem.əˌræn.dəm ˈn ˌaː.tɪ.klz əv ə.səʊ.siˈeɪ.ʃən/ 20
merge /mɜːdʒ/ 27
merger inquiry /ˈmɜː.dʒər ɪnˌkwaɪə.ri/ 28
merger /ˈmɜː.dʒər/ 9, 27
mini-pupillage /ˌmɪn.i ˈpjuː.pəl.ɪdʒ/ 10
minimum authorised share capital /ˌmɪn.ɪ.məm ˌɔː.θər.aɪzd ˈʃeər ˌkæp.ɪ.tˈl/ 19
minor /ˈmaɪ.nər/ 4, 32
minutes /ˈmɪn.ɪts/ 11, 23
misleading /ˌmɪsˈliː.dɪŋ/ 28, 43
misrepresentation /mɪs.rep.rɪ.zenˈteɪ.ʃən/ 34, 36, 43, 44
monetary penalty /ˈmʌn.ɪ.tri ˌpen.ˈl.ti/ 28
monetary value /ˈmʌn.ɪ.tri ˌvæl.juː/ 6
money laundering /ˈmʌn.i ˌlɔːn.drɪŋ/ 15, 44
monitor workloads /ˌmɒn.ɪ.tə ˈwɜːk.ləʊdz/ 13
monitoring /ˈmɒn.ɪ.tˈr.ɪŋ/ 45
monopoly power /məˈnɒp.əl.i ˌpaʊər/ 28
mortgage (n) /ˈmɔː.gɪdʒ/ 20, 22
mortgage (v) /ˈmɔː.gɪdʒ/ 20, 22
mortgagee /ˌmɔː.gɪˈdʒiː/ 22
multi track /ˌmʌl.tiˈtræk/ 6
multiple systems /ˌmʌl.tɪ.pl ˈsɪs.təmz/ 38
mutual assistance in policing /ˌmjuː.tʃu.əl əˌsɪs.tˈnts ɪn pəˈliː.sɪŋ/ 44
national /ˈnæʃ.ˈn.ˈl/ 8
national law /ˌnæʃ.ˈn.ˈl ˈlɔː/ 8
national sovereignty /ˌnæʃ.ˈn.ˈl ˈsɒv.rɪn.ti/ 8

negligence /'neg.lɪ.dʒᵊnts/ 29, 30, 35

negotiate detailed terms /nə,gəʊ.ʃi.eɪt ˌdiː.teɪld 'tɜːmz/ 40

no win no fee /,nəʊ ,wɪn ,nəʊ 'fiː/ 30

nominal capital /,nɒm.ɪ.nəl 'kæp.ɪ.tᵊl/ 21

nominal value /,nɒm.ɪ.nəl 'væl.juː/ 21, 31

nominated to receive disclosures /,nɒm.ɪ.neɪ.tɪd tə rɪ,siːv dɪ'skləʊ.ʒəz/ 15

non-binding instruments /,nɒn.baɪn.dɪŋ 'ɪn.strə.mənts/ 45

non-cash consideration /,nɒn. kæʃ kən.sɪd.ə'reɪ.ʃᵊn/ 21

non-compliance with /,nɒn.kəm'plaɪ.ənts wɪð/ 28

non-contentious litigation /,nɒn.kən.tent.ʃəs lɪt.ɪ'geɪ.ʃᵊn/ 6

non-exclusive /,nɒn.ɪk'skluː.sɪv/ 38

non-exhaustive illustrations /,nɒn.ɪg.zɔː.stɪv ɪl.ə'streɪ.ʃᵊnz/ 35

non-obvious /,nɒn'ɒb.vi.əs/ 42

non-practising /,nɒn 'præk.tɪ.sɪŋ/ 10

not be liable whatsoever /,nɒt biː ,laɪ.ə.bl wɒt.səʊ'ev.əʳ/ 35

not guilty plea /,nɒt 'gɪl.ti ,pliː/ 5

notice of change /,nəʊ.tɪs əv 'tʃeɪndʒ/ 23

notice of termination of employment /,nəʊ.tɪs əv tɜː.mɪ,neɪ.ʃᵊn əv ɪm'plɔɪ.mənt/ 41

notifiable offence /,nəʊ.tɪ.faɪ.ə.bl ə'fents/ 5

notify /'nəʊ.tɪ.faɪ/ 26

notwithstanding /,nɒt.wɪð'stæn.dɪŋ/ 18

novation /nəʊ 'veɪ.ʃᵊn/ 36

novel /'nɒv.ᵊl/ 42

nuisance /'njuː.sᵊnts/ 29

objects /'ɒb.dʒekts/ 20

obligation on /,ɒb.lɪ'geɪ.ʃᵊn ɒn/ 8

obligations under contract /ɒb.lɪ,geɪ.ʃᵊnz ʌn.də 'kɒn.trækt/ 36

obsolete /'ɒb.sᵊ.liːt/ 2

obtain a degree /əb,teɪn ə dɪ'griː/ 9

obtain approval /əb,teɪn ə'pruː.vᵊl/ 14

obtain by deception /əb,teɪn baɪ dɪ'sep.ʃᵊn/ 44

obtain consent to the assignment /əb,teɪn kən,sent tuː ðiː ə'saɪn.mənt/ 39

obtain medical records /əb'teɪn ,med.ɪ.kᵊl ,re.kɔːdz/ 30

occupation /,ɒk.jʊ'peɪ.ʃᵊn/ 39

occupational pension scheme /,ɒk.jʊ.peɪ.ʃᵊn.ᵊl 'pent.ʃᵊn ,skiːm/ 24

occupier /'ɒk.jʊ.paɪ.əʳ/ 39

offence /ə'fents/ 28

offence under this regulation /ə,fents ʌn.də ðɪs reg.jʊ'leɪ.ʃᵊn/ 15

offender /ə'fen.dəʳ/ 1, 5

offer (n) /'ɒf.əʳ/ 31, 37

offer (v) /'ɒf.əʳ/ 13

offeree /,ɒf.ə'riː/ 27, 31

offeror /,ɒf.ə'rɔː/ 27, 31

Office for Harmonisation in the Internal Market (OHIM) /,ɒf.ɪs fɔːr hɑː.mə.na ɪ,zeɪ.ʃᵊn ɪn ðə ɪn,tɜː.nəl 'mɑː.kɪt/ 43

office manual /,ɒf.ɪs 'mæn.ju.əl/ 14

on behalf of /ɒn bɪ'hɑːf ɒv/ 16, 24, 36

on secondment /ɒn sɪ'kɒnd.mənt/ 9

on the seller's terms /ɒn ðə 'sel.əz ,tɜːmz/ 37

one-off transaction /,wʌn.ɒf træn'zæk.ʃᵊn/ 15

operative clause /,ɒp.ᵊr.ə.tɪv 'klɔːz/ 33

operative provisions /,ɒp.ᵊr.ə.tɪv prə'vɪʒ.ᵊnz/ 33

opinion /ə'pɪn.jən/ 8, 30

orally /'ɔː.rə.li/ 32

original /ə'rɪdʒ.ɪ.nəl/ 43

original jurisdiction /ə,rɪdʒ.ɪ.nəl dʒʊə.rɪs'dɪk.ʃᵊn/ 4

original work /ə,rɪdʒ.ɪ.nəl 'wɜːk/ 42

out of office message /,aʊt əv 'ɒf.ɪs ,mes.ɪdʒ/ 11

outcome /'aʊt.kʌm/ 30

outside /,aʊt'saɪd/ 35

overall responsibility for /,əʊ.və.rɔːl rɪ.spɒnt.sɪ'bɪl.ɪ.ti fɔːʳ/ 14

override /,əʊ.və'raɪd/ 3, 37

owe to /'əʊ tuː/ 29

pain and suffering /,peɪn ᵊn 'sʌf.ᵊr.ɪŋ/ 29

par value /'pɑːr ,væl.juː/ 21

paralegals /'pær.ə,liː.gəlz/ 11

part-time /,pɑːt'taɪm/ 41

partial performance /,pɑː.ʃᵊl pə'fɔː.mənts/ 36

particulars /pə'tɪk.jʊ.ləz/ 6

parties concerned /,pɑː.tiz kən'sɜːnd/ 31

partly performed /'pɑːt.li pə'fɔːmd/ 36

partner /'pɑːt.nəʳ/ 9, 11, 19

partner-led team /'pɑːt.nə led ,tiːm/ 13

Partnership Agreement /'pɑːt.nə.ʃɪp ə,griː.mənt/ 19

partnership /'pɑːt.nə.ʃɪp/ 9, 19, 26

party /'pɑː.ti/ 7, 12, 32, 33

pass /pɑːs/ 40

pass an Act /,pɑːs ən 'ækt/ 2

passing off /,pɑː.sɪŋ 'ɒf/ 43

patent /'peɪ.tᵊnt/ 42

patent application /'peɪ.tᵊnt æp.lɪ,keɪ.ʃᵊn/ 42

patent holder /,peɪ.tᵊnt 'həʊl.dəʳ/ 42

patentable /'peɪ.tᵊntə.bl/ 42

payment schedule /'peɪ.mənt ,ʃed.juːl/ 30

penal establishment /'piː.nəl ɪ,stæb.lɪʃ.mənt/ 12

penalties arise /'pen.ᵊl.tiz ə,raɪz/ 40

penalty /'pen.əl.ti/ 40

per pro /'pɜː ,prəʊ/ 18

per se /'pɜː ,seɪ/ 18

perform a condition /pə,fɔːm ə kən'dɪʃ.ᵊn/ 34

perform the contract /pə,fɔːm ðə 'kɒn.trækt/ 32, 34

permissions /pə'mɪʃ.ᵊnz/ 38

permit /pə'mɪt/ 38

permitted use /pə,mɪ.tɪd 'juːs/ 38

person accused /,pɜː.sᵊn ə'kjuːzd/ 5

personal assets /,pɜː.sᵊn.ᵊl 'æs.ets/ 19

personal data /,pɜː.sᵊn.ᵊl 'deɪ.tə/ 44

personal injury /,pɜː.sᵊn.ᵊl 'ɪn.dʒᵊr.i/ 29

persons /'pɜː.sᵊnz/ 8, 23

persuasive /pə'sweɪ.sɪv/ 8

persuasive authority /pə,sweɪ.sɪv ɔː'θɒr.ɪ.ti/ 3

petition the court /pə,tɪʃ.ᵊn ðə 'kɔːt/ 24

petty crime /,pet.i 'kraɪm/ 4

pharming /'fɑː.mɪŋ/ 44

phishing /'fɪ.ʃɪŋ/ 44

placement /'pleɪs.mənt/ 9

plaintiff /'pleɪn.tɪf/ 4, 6, 29

planning permission /'plæn.ɪŋ pə,mɪʃ.ᵊn/ 40

plead guilty /,pliːd 'gɪl.ti/ 5

please find enclosed /,pliːz ,faɪnd ɪn'kləʊzd/ 16

pledge /pledʒ/ 22

points of law /,pɔɪnts əv 'lɔː/ 4

policing /pə'liː.sɪŋ/ 44

polluter pays principle /pə,luː.tə 'peɪz ,prɪnt.sɪ.pl/ 45

pollution control laws /pə,luː.ʃᵊn kən'trəʊl ,lɔːz/ 45

postal acceptance rule /,pəʊ.stᵊl ək'sep.tᵊnts ,ruːl/ 31

postgraduate Diploma in Law (GDL) /,pəʊst.grædʒ.u.ət dɪ,pləʊ.mə ɪn 'lɔː/ 10

potential claim /pəʊ,ten.tʃᵊl 'kleɪm/ 30

practicable /'præk.tɪ.kə.bl/ 15

practice /'præk.tɪs/ 9, 43

practice directions /,præk.tɪs daɪ'rek.ʃᵊnz/ 6

practise /'præk.tɪs/ 3, 9

practise at the Bar /,præk.tɪs æt ðə 'bɑːʳ/ 10

pre-conditions /,priː.kən'dɪʃ.ənz/ 33

pre-contract enquiries /,priː.kɒn.trækt ɪn'kwaɪə.riz/ 40

pre-emption /,pri'emp.ʃᵊn/ 21

Pre-Qualification Questionnaire (PPQ) /,pri.kwɒl.ɪ.fɪ.keɪ.ʃᵊn kwes.tʃə'neəʳ/ 13

preamble /'priː.æm.bl/ 33

precautionary principle /prɪ,kɔː.ʃᵊn.ᵊr.i 'prɪnt.sɪ.pl/ 45

precedent letters /'pres.ɪ.dᵊnt ,let.ərz/ 14

preceding transaction /prɪ,siː.dɪŋ træn'zæk.ʃᵊn/ 33

predatory pricing /,pred.ə.tᵊr.i 'praɪ.sɪŋ/ 28

preferential creditor /,pref.ᵊr.en.t ʃᵊl 'kred.ɪ.təʳ/ 24

preparatory hearing /prɪ'pær.ᵊ.tər.i ,hɪə.rɪŋ/ 5

prepare a report /prɪ,peəʳ ə rɪ'pɔːt/ 30

prepare the first draft /prɪ,peə ðə ,fɜːst 'drɑːft/ 14

prepared as if /prɪ'peəd æz ɪf/ 14

pressure group /'preʃ.ə ,gruːp/ 2

prevail /prɪ'veɪl/ 35

previous dealings /,priː.vi.əs 'diː.lɪŋz/ 34

prima facie /,praɪ.mə'feɪ.ʃi/ 18

primary legislation /,praɪ.mə.ri ledʒ.ɪs'leɪ.ʃᵊn/ 2

principal /'prɪnt.sɪ.pᵊl/ 36

principle of binding precedent /,prɪnt.sɪ.pl əv ,baɪn.dɪŋ 'pres.ɪ.dənt/ 3

prior written consent /,praɪə ,rɪt.ᵊn kən'sent/ 35

Private Act /'praɪ.vət ,ækt/ 2

Private Client /'praɪ.vət ,klaɪ.ᵊnt/ 13

Private Finance Initiative (PFI) /,praɪ.vət 'faɪ.nænts ɪ,nɪʃ.ə.tɪv/ 11, 13

private law /'praɪ.vət ,lɔː/ 1

Private Limited Company (Ltd) /'praɪ.vət ,lɪm.ɪ.tɪd 'kʌm.pə.ni/ 19

Private Members Bill /,praɪ.vət 'mem.bəz ,bɪl/ 2

privatisation /,praɪ.vɪ.taɪ'zeɪ.ʃᵊn/ 9

privity of contract /,prɪvəti əv 'kɒn.trækt/ 36

pro rata /,prəʊ'rɑː.tə/ 18

probation officer /prəʊ'beɪ.ʃᵊn ,ɒf.ɪ.səʳ/ 12

Probation Service /prəʊ'beɪ.ʃᵊn ,sɜː.vɪs/ 12

procedural judge /prə'siː.djuː.rəl ,dʒʌdʒ/ 6

procedural law /prə'siː.djuː.rəl ,lɔː/ 1

procedure /prə'siː.dʒəʳ/ 16, 17

proceed to sentence /prəʊ,siːd tə 'sen.tənts/ 5

proceeds of /'prəʊ.siːdz ɒv/ 15

procure the satisfaction of the condition /prə,kjʊə ðə sæt.ɪs,fæk.ʃᵊn əv ðə kən'dɪʃ.ᵊn/ 33

procurement /prə'kjʊə.mənt/ 13

product defects /,prɒd.ʌkt 'diː.fekts/ 29

produce satisfactory evidence /prə,djuːs ,sæt.ɪs,fæk.tᵊr.i 'ev.ɪ.dᵊnts/ 15

produce uniformity /prə,djuːs juː.nɪ'fɔː.mɪ.ti/ 37

profess /prə'fes/ 38

professional body /prə,feʃ.ᵊn.ᵊl 'bɒd.i/ 2

professional indemnity cover /prə,feʃ.ᵊn.ᵊl ɪn'dem.nə.ti ,kʌv.əʳ/ 13

profits /'prɒf.ɪtz/ 26

proof of title /,pruːf əv 'taɪ.tl/ 40

property /'prɒp.ə.ti/ 22, 39, 40

property interest /'prɒp.ə.ti ,ɪn.tᵊr.est/ 42

property of the Crown /,prɒp.ə.ti əv ðə 'kraʊn/ 23

property particulars /,prɒp.ə.ti pə'tɪk.jʊ.ləz/ 40

proposal /prə'pəʊ.zᵊl/ 2

propose a bill /prə,pəʊz ə 'bɪl/ 2

proprietor /prə'praɪə.təʳ/ 43

prosecute /'prɒs.ɪ.kjuːt/ 1, 4, 5

protect best interests /prə,tekt best 'ɪn.tᵊr.ests/ 11

protect the environment /prə,tekt ðiː ɪn'vaɪə.rən.mənt/ 45

protected /prə'tek.tɪd/ 38, 43

prove beyond reasonable doubt /,pruːv bi.jɒnd ,riː.zᵊn.ə.bl 'daʊt/ 5

provide (details) /prə'vaɪd/ 23

(clause) provides that /prə'vaɪdz ðæt/ 36

provide a comprehensive service to /prə,vaɪd ə ,kɒm.prɪ'hent.sɪv 'sɜː.vɪs tuː/ 13

provide a fee estimate /prə,vaɪd ə ,fiː 'es.tɪ.mət/ 14

provide replies to /prə,vaɪd rɪ'plaɪz tuː/ 40

provide representation /prə,vaɪd rep.rɪ.zen'teɪ.ʃᵊn/ 10

provision of /prə'vɪʒ.ᵊn ɒv/ 13

provisions /prə'vɪʒ.ᵊnz/ 8, 33, 35, 37

public access to information /,pʌb.lɪk ,æk.ses tu ɪn.fə'meɪ.ʃᵊn/ 45

Public Act /,pʌb.lɪk 'ækt/ 2

public law /,pʌb.lɪk 'lɔː/ 1

Public Limited Company (PLC) /,pʌb.lɪk ,lɪm.ɪ.tɪd 'kʌm.pə.ni/ 19

public participation /,pʌb.lɪk pɑː.tɪs.ɪ'peɪ.ʃᵊn/ 45

public prosecutor /,pʌb.lɪk 'prɒs.ɪ.kjuː.təʳ/ 5

public purse /,pʌb.lɪk 'pɜːs/ 7

public scrutiny /,pʌb.lɪk 'skruː.tɪ.ni/ 2

Public Sector /'pʌb.lɪk ,sek.təʳ/ 11

pupil master /'pjuː.pᵊl ,mɑː.stəʳ/ 10

pupillage /'pjuː.pəl.ɪdʒ/ 10

purchase /'pɜː.tʃəs/ 40

rule at law reasoned /ˌruːl ət ˈlɔː ˌriː.zᵊnd/ 3

sale agreement /ˈseɪl əˌgriː.mənt/ 31, 40

sale by auction /ˌseɪl baɪ ˈɔːk.ʃᵊn/ 40

sale by private treaty /ˌseɪl baɪ ˌpraɪ.vət ˈtriː.ti/ 40

sale memorandum /ˌseɪl ˈmem.əˈræn.dəm/ 40

(the) same /seɪm/ 16

satisfactory evidence /sæt.ɪsˌfæk.tᵊr.i ˈev.ɪ.dᵊnts/ 15

satisfy pre-conditions /ˌsæt.ɪs.faɪ priː.kənˈdɪʃ.ᵊnz/ 33

schedule /ˈʃed.juːl/ 33

scrutinise the provisions /ˌskruː.tɪ.naɪz ðə prəˈvɪʒ.ᵊnz/ 2

seal /siːl/ 32

search /sɜːtʃ/ 40

search order /ˌsɜːtʃ ˈɔː.dəʳ/ 43

second essential leg /ˌsek.ᵊnd ɪˌsen.t ʃᵊl ˈleg/ 30

secondary legislation /ˌsek.ᵊn.dri ledʒ.ɪˈsleɪ.ʃᵊn/ 2, 8

secured creditor /sɪˌkjʊərd ˈkred.ɪ.təʳ/ 22, 24

secured lending /sɪˌkjʊərd ˈlen.dɪŋ/ 22

security /sɪˈkjʊə.rɪ.ti/ 19, 22

security provisions /sɪˈkjʊə.rɪ.ti prəˌvɪʒ.ᵊnz/ 39

security system /sɪˈkjʊə.rɪ.ti ˌsɪs.təm/ 44

seek a legal remedy /ˌsiːk ə ˌliː.gᵊl ˈrem.ə.di/ 4

seek an injunction /ˌsiːk ən ɪnˈdʒʌŋk.ʃᵊn/ 12

seek medical advice /ˌsiːk ˈmed.ɪ.kᵊl ədˌvaɪs/ 30

seek to exclude /ˌsiːk tu ɪkˈskluːd/ 35

self-employed practice /ˌself. ɪmˌplɔɪd ˈpræk.tɪs/ 10

seller /ˈsel.əʳ/ 40

seller's terms /ˈsel.əz ˌtɜːmz/ 37

send acceptance /ˌsend əkˈsep.tᵊnts/ 31

senior barrister /ˌsiː.ni.ə ˈbær.ɪ.stəʳ/ 10

sentence /ˈsen.tənts/ 4, 5

sentencing /ˈsen.tənt.sɪŋ/ 12

series of law reports /ˌsɪə.riːz əv ˈlɔː rɪˌpɔːts/ 3

serve a summons /ˌsɜːv ə ˈsʌm.ənz/ 5

serve notice /ˌsɜːv ˈnəʊ.tɪs/ 39

serve on /ˈsɜːv ɒn/ 6, 23

serve with /ˈsɜːv wɪð/ 23

service contract /ˈsɜː.vɪs ˌkɒn.trækt/ 31

service mark /ˈsɜː.vɪs ˌmɑːk/ 43

services /ˈsɜː.vɪs.ɪz/ 8

(a) set /set/ 10

set a timetable /ˌset ə ˈtaɪm.teɪ.bl̩/ 6

set aside /ˌset əˈsaɪd/ 32

set out /ˌset ˈaʊt/ 2, 34

set out in /ˌset ˈaʊt ɪn/ 14, 24

set the precedent /ˌset ðə ˈpres.ɪ.dᵊnt/ 3

settle a claim /ˌset.l ə ˈkleɪm/ 29

settle differences /ˌset.l ˈdɪf.ᵊr.ᵊnt.sɪz/ 6

settlement /ˈset.l.mənt/ 25

settlement of disputes /ˌset.l.mənt əv dɪˈspjuːts/ 41

severance clause /ˈsev.ᵊr.ənts ˌklɔːz/ 35

severe penalty /sɪˌvɪə ˈpen.ᵊl.ti/ 5

shadow /ˈʃæd.əʊ/ 10

shall /ʃæl/ 17

share capital /ˈʃeə ˌkæp.ɪ.təl/ 20, 21

share certificate /ˈʃeə səˌtɪf.ɪ.kət/ 21

share transaction /ˈʃeə træn.zæk.ʃən/ 27

share value /ˈʃeə ˌvæl.juː/ 21

shareholder /ˈʃeəˌhəʊl.dəʳ/ 19, 20, 24

shareholding /ˈʃeəˌhəʊl.dɪŋ/ 21

shares /ʃeəz/ 19

shares issued /ˌʃeəz ˈɪʃ.uːd/ 20

shelf company /ˈʃelf ˌkʌm.pə.ni/ 20

shrink-wrap license /ˈʃrɪŋk.ræp ˌlaɪ.sᵊnts/ 38

sick pay /ˈsɪk ˌpeɪ/ 41

sign /saɪn/ 43

signatory of /ˈsɪg.nə.tri əv/ 1

significant proportion of /sɪgˌnɪf.ɪ.kənt prəˈpɔː.ʃᵊn əv/ 11

similar to /ˈsɪm.ɪ.lə tuː/ 17

simple contract /ˌsɪm.pl ˈkɒn.trækt/ 32

Single European Act (1986) /ˌsɪŋ.gl jʊə.rəˈpiː.ən ˌækt/ 8

Single Internal Market /ˌsɪŋ.gl ɪn.tɜː.nᵊl ˈmɑː.kɪt/ 8

sister firm /ˈsɪs.tə ˌfɜːm/ 14

sit separately /ˌsɪt ˈsep.ᵊr.ət.li/ 1

sitting /ˈsɪt.ɪŋ/ 4

slander /ˈslɑːn.dəʳ/ 29

sleeping partner /ˌsliː.pɪŋ ˈpɑːt.nəʳ/ 19

small claims /ˌsmɔːl ˈkleɪmz/ 6

society /səˈsaɪ.ə.ti/ 26

sold by auction /ˌsəʊld baɪ ˈɔːk.ʃᵊn/ 40

sold by private treaty /ˌsəʊld baɪ ˌpraɪ.vət ˈtriː.ti/ 40

sole trader /ˌsəʊl ˈtreɪ.dəʳ/ 10, 19

solicitor /səˈlɪs.ɪ.təʳ/ 9

solvent /ˈsɒl.vənt/ 24

sound file /ˌsaʊnd ˈfaɪl/ 11

source /sɔːs/ 43

special damages /ˌspeʃ.ᵊl ˈdæm.ɪ.dʒɪz/ 29

special expertise /ˌspeʃ.ᵊl ek.spɜːˈtiːz/ 7

specialise in /ˈspeʃ.əl.aɪz ɪn/ 9

specialism /ˈspeʃ.ᵊl.ɪ.zᵊm/ 9

specialist /ˈspeʃ.ᵊl.ɪst/ 13

specified in /ˈspes.ɪ.faɪd ɪn/ 15

specialist knowledge /ˌspeʃ.ᵊl.ɪst ˈnɒl.ɪdʒ/ 13

specified monetary sums /ˌspes.ɪ.faɪd ˌmʌn.ɪ.tri ˈsʌmz/ 6

standard clause /ˌstæn.dəd ˈklɔːz/ 35

standard conditions /ˌstæn.dəd kənˈdɪʃ.ᵊnz/ 37

standard terms /ˌstæn.dəd ˈtɜːmz/ 37

standard wording /ˌstæn.dəd ˈwɜː.dɪŋ/ 32

statements of law /ˌsteɪt.mənts əv ˈlɔː/ 3

statute /ˈstæ.tʃuːt/ 2

statute law /ˌstæ.tʃuːt ˈlɔː/ 1

statutory books /ˌstæ.tjʊ.tᵊr.i ˈbʊks/ 20

statutory forms /ˌstæ.tjʊ.tᵊr.i ˈfɔːmz/ 23

statutory instruments /ˌstæ.tjʊ.tᵊr.i ˈɪn.strə.mənts/ 2

statutory notices /ˌstæ.tjʊ.tᵊr.i ˈnəʊ.tɪs.ɪz/ 23

statutory period /ˌstæ.tjʊ.tᵊr.i ˈpɪə.ri.əd/ 42

statutory provisions /ˌstæ.tjʊ.tᵊr.i prəˈvɪʒ.ᵊnz/ 37

statutory regime /ˌstæ.tjʊ.tᵊr.i reɪˈʒiːm/ 39

statutory regulations /ˌstæ.tjʊ.tᵊr.i reg.jʊˈleɪ.ʃᵊnz/ 45

statutory rights /ˌstæ.tjʊ.tᵊr.i ˈraɪts/ 41

Trading Certificate /ˌtreɪ.dɪŋ səˈtɪf.ɪ.kət/ 19

trading entity /ˌtreɪ.dɪŋ ˈen.tɪ.ti/ 19

trading goodwill /ˌtreɪ.dɪŋ ɡʊdˈwɪl/ 43

trading name /ˈtreɪ.dɪŋ ˌneɪm/ 20

trading vehicle /ˈtreɪ.dɪŋ ˌviː.ɪ.kl/ 19

trainee /ˌtreɪˈniː/ 9, 10

traineeship /treɪˈniː.ʃɪp/ 9

training /ˈtreɪ.nɪŋ/ 9, 10, 12

training contract /ˈtreɪ.nɪŋ ˌkɒn.trækt/ 9

transaction /trænˈzæk.ʃ°n/ 15, 37

transfer interest in /trænsˌfɜːʳ ˈɪn.t°r.est ɪn/ 39

transfer know-how into / trænsˌfɜː ˈnəʊ.haʊ ˌɪn.tuː/ 13

transfer of business /trænsˌfɜːr əv ˈbɪz.nɪs/ 41

transfer of title /trænsˌfɜːr əv ˈtaɪ.tl/ 22

transfer shares /trænsˌfɜːr ˈʃeəz/ 20

transposed into /trænˈspəʊzd ˌɪn.tuː/ 8

treat as /ˈtriːt æz/ 24, 32, 34

treaty /ˈtriː.ti/ 45

Treaty on European Union (TEU) /ˌtriː.ti ɒn ˌjʊə.rə.piː.ən ˈjuː.ni.ən/ 8

trespass /ˈtres.pəs/ 29

triable either way /ˈtraɪ.ə.bl ˌaɪðə ˌweɪ/ 5

trial by jury /ˌtraɪəl baɪ ˈdʒʊə.ri/ 5

tribunal /traɪˈbjuː.nəl/ 7

try summarily /ˌtraɪ ˈsʌm.er.ɪ.li/ 4

turn out to be /ˌtɜːn ˈaʊt tə biː/ 34

type up /ˌtaɪp ˈʌp/ 11

typography /taɪˈpɒɡ.rə.fi/ 42

ultra vires /ˌʌl.trə ˈvɪə.reɪz/ 18

unauthorised access to /ʌnˌɔː.θə.raɪzd ˈæk.ses tuː/ 44

under an Act /ˌʌn.dər ən ˈækt/ 1

under arrest /ˌʌn.dər əˈrest/ 5

under no liability /ˌʌn.də ˈnəʊ laɪ.əˌbɪl.ɪ.ti/ 35

under-tenant /ˈʌn.də.ten.ənt/ 39

under the terms of /ˌʌn.də ðə ˈtɜːmz ɒv/ 38

undergo medical treatment /ˌʌn.də.ɡəʊ ˈmed.ɪ.kᵉl ˌtriːt.ment/ 29

underlet /ˌʌn.dəˈlet/ 39

(the) undermentioned 18 /ˌʌn.dəˈmen.tʃənd/

undertake (drafting of legislation) /ˌʌn.dəˈteɪk/ 2

undertake work /ˌʌn.də.teɪk ˈwɜːk/ 9, 14

undertaking /ˌʌn.dəˈteɪ.kɪŋ/ 12, 28

undischarged bankrupt /ʌn.dɪsˌtʃɑːdʒd ˈbæŋ.krʌpt/ 23

unenforceable /ˌʌn.ɪnˈfɔː.sə.bl/ 32, 35

unfair contract terms /ʌnˌfeə ˈkɒn.trækt ˌtɜːmz/ 35

unfair dismissal /ʌnˌfeə dɪˈsmɪs.əl/ 7, 41

uniformity /ˌjuː.nɪˈfɔː.mɪ.ti/ 37

unilaterally varied /ˌjuː.nɪˈlæt.ᵉr.ᵉl.i ˈveə.rɪd/ 41

unlawful deductions /ʌnˌlɔː.fᵉl dɪˈdʌk.ʃᵉnz/ 41

unlimited liability /ʌnˌlɪm.ɪ.tɪd laɪ.əˈbɪl.ɪ.ti/ 10

unliquidated damages /ʌnˌlɪk.wɪ.deɪ.tɪd ˈdæm.ɪ.dʒɪz/ 36

unqualified agreement /ʌnˌkwɒl.ɪ.faɪd əˈgriː.mənt/ 31

unsecured creditor /ˌʌn.sɪ.kjʊəd ˈkred.ɪ.təʳ/ 24

update legislation /ʌpˈdeɪt ˌledʒ.ɪˈsleɪ.ʃən/ 2

updated /ʌpˈdeɪ.tɪd/ 14

uphold a decision /ʌpˌhəʊld ə dɪˈsɪʒ.ᵉn/ 4

upper house /ˌʌp.ə ˈhaʊs/ 1

use and enjoyment of /ˌjuːs ᵉn ɪnˈdʒɔɪ.mənt əv/ 29

use by multiple systems /ˌjuːz baɪ ˌmʌl.tɪ.pl ˈsɪs.təmz/ 38

use discretion to /ˌjuːz dɪsˈkreʃ.ᵉn tuː/ 36

vague /veɪg/ 31

valuation /ˌvæl.juˈeɪ.ʃᵉn/ 22

vary /ˈveə.ri/ 41

variation of contract /ˌveə.riˈeɪ.ʃᵉn əv ˈkɒn.trækt/ 41

verdict /ˈvɜː.dɪkt/ 5

vested in /ˈves.tɪd ɪn/ 42

vice versa /ˌvaɪsˈvɜː.sə/ 33

virus spreading /ˈvaɪə.rəs ˌspre.dɪŋ/ 44

virus writing /ˈvaɪə.rəs ˌraɪ.tɪŋ/ 44

viz (videlicet) /vɪz/ 18

void /vɔɪd/ 27, 32

voidable /ˈvɔɪ.də.bl/ 32

voluntary liquidation /ˌvɒl.ən.tri ˌlɪk.wɪˈdeɪ.ʃᵉn/ 24

voluntary organisation /ˈvɒl.ən.tri ɔː.gᵉn.aˌɪ.zeɪ.ʃᵉn/ 2

voluntary self-regulatory code /ˌvɒl.ən.tri ˌself reg.jʊˈleɪ.tᵉr.i ˌkaʊd/ 27

vote on resolutions /ˈvəʊt ɒn rez.əˈluː.ʃᵉnz/ 21

wage /weɪdʒ/ 41

waive /weɪv/ 23

warrant of arrest /ˌwɒr.ᵉnt əv əˈrest/ 5

warranty /ˈwɒr.ᵉn.ti/ 33, 34, 37, 40

where /weəʳ/ 34

whereas /weəˈræz/ 33

whereby /weəˈbaɪ/ 33

will /wɪl/ 9

winding up order /ˌwaɪn.dɪŋ ˈʌp ˌɔː.dəʳ/ 24

World Intellectual Property Organization (WIPO) /ˌwɜːld ɪn.tᵉl.ek.tju.əl ˈprɒp.ə.ti ɔː.gᵉn.aɪˌzeɪ.ʃᵉn/ 43

with the assistance of /wɪð ðiː əˈsɪs.tᵉnts ɒv/ 24

withdraw a claim /wɪðˌdrɔː ə ˈkleɪm/ 7

within /wɪˈðɪn/ 30, 34

within the requisite period /wɪˌðɪn ðə ˌrek.wɪ.zɪt ˈpɪə.ri.əd/ 23

without lawful justification /wɪˌðaʊt ˌlɔː.fəl dʒʌs.tɪ.fɪˈkeɪ.ʃᵉn/ 29

without the consent of /wɪˌðaʊt ðə kənˈsent ɒv/ 36

witness statement /ˈwɪt.nəs ˌsteɪt.mənt/ 6, 7

witness /ˈwɪt.nəs/ 5

wound up /ˌwaʊnd ˈʌp/ 21

writ of summons /rɪt əv ˈsʌm.ənz/ 6

written constitution /ˌrɪt.ᵉn kɒn.stɪˈtjuː.ʃᵉn/ 1

wrong /rɒŋ/ 29

wrongful dismissal /ˌrɒŋ.fəl dɪsˈmɪs.ᵉl/ 41

yield up /ˌjiːld ˈʌp/ 39